On the Road: The Marathon

On the Road: The Marathon

by
Jim Shapiro

*with photographs by
Joe Greene*

Crown Publishers, Inc.
New York

Inquiries should be addressed to Crown Publishers, Inc., One Park Avenue, New York, N.Y. 10016

Published simultaneously in Canada by General Publishing Company Limited

Printed in the United States of America

Designed by Jon M. Nelson

Library of Congress Cataloging in Publication Data

Shapiro, Jim.
  On the road.
  Bibliography: p.
  1. Marathon running. I. Title.
GV1065.S42 1978   796.4'26   78-13331
ISBN 0-517-53443-6
ISBN 0-517-53444-4 pbk.

To my mother and father

Running brings health and joy. It is like air, like earth.

—MIKI GORMAN

You should not be a smoky fire. You should burn yourself completely.

—SHUNRYU SUZUKI,
Zen Mind, Beginner's Mind

Je n'aime pas l'homme; j'aime ce qui le dévore.

—ANDRÉ GIDE

Contents

Preface

Marathon running is a microcosm of the world. Anything to which one totally commits oneself betrays the deepest attitudes and convictions. The inevitable difficulties one encounters in training for a marathon—the long stretch of roadway and the intense effort expended to complete the course—flush to the surface true feelings, true desires, true faces. The sport itself is comparatively young, having begun in 1896 and not really having exploded into anything near its present popularity until a few years ago. Already stories of great drama, of heroes past and present, are legendary. But the sport is primarily a private one, even for those like Shorter, Zatopek, and Mimoun, who have been drenched in public glory.

This book examines the history of these footraces, whether of marathon length or longer; it is the story of those who love and endure them—the hardships they face and the motivations that sustain them—and the various facets of the sport that have emerged and changed over the years. As with any other sport, marathoning reflects the culture that nurtures it. Technology, scientific research, mass numbers of participants, media exposure, fashion, marathoning as a full-time vocation—these recent and important developments will, to some extent, determine its direction not only now but also in the future.

Marathon running is an art form as demanding as any other. The motivations run deep, the running itself is too special and dreamlike ever to be completely mined. The sport, perhaps because of the pain involved, needs a voice in order to find reasons for such intense devotion. For there are reasons why people run the marathon no matter how imperfectly they are understood or expressed.

Most of the voices you will hear in these pages are American, since it was not possible to travel around the world to interview the many dedicated and zealous runners. However, I believe the differences among runners are individual ones, not ones that can be attributed to differences in nationality. Marathoners understand one another and the demands of their sport clearly enough, regardless of background. I have tried to illustrate these personal diversities by sampling, not by attempting the impossible and including everyone. My own experiences in running and my own temperament obviously affected the emphasis of the book. It is not meant to be a handbook or text offering helpful hints for improving running performance, nor is it a statistician's catalog. The experience of marathon running, the intensity of it, its meaning, and what is left afterward for the runner to remember and distill from it—this is the book's deepest concern. Nevertheless, this book can render only a partial truth. Where one was in the middle of a race changes as irrevocably as the flashing of feet over asphalt—never to be repeated or understood with more than partial precision.

Acknowledgments

I would like to thank a few of those who encouraged and helped Joe and me along the way: Max and Jenny White, Virginia Armat, Ted Corbitt, Sharon Zane, Jennifer Gerard-Maric, Christine Costa, Sue Snyder, and Fred Rothberg. Fellow runners Richard Innamorato, Mike Cleary, Richard Langsam, John McBride, and John Cederholm were helpful in their different ways. Dr. Edward Colt, an endocrinologist at St. Luke's Hospital in New York City, very kindly reviewed portions of the manuscript. Jock Semple, an early mentor, also gave generously of his time and attention.

Special thanks go to our families as well, for their perpetual support.

And thanks are extended to Yaddo, an artist's colony in Saratoga Springs, New York, where some of this book was written.

J.E.S.

1

O Marathon!

Every four years, at the Olympics somewhere in the world, a group of highly specialized young men, marathon runners—that is, artists, jugglers of the mundane and spiritual, craftsmen, poets of the flesh, stinking of sweat and Ben-Gay—gather on a track under the eyes of the world. No one except for the cattle trucks of news photographers or TV cameramen will get to follow them the whole way. Everyone else waits in the stands or sits at home in front of a TV, far removed from the action. You can only watch these runners and try to imagine what they must be feeling. But "running is running," as Frank Shorter insists, and certainly, on the afternoon of the Olympic marathon, nothing else matters but the doing of it. In the brief time left there is little energy for the kind of teasing camaraderie apparent in other marathons. In 1976 the three American marathoners had never gotten together as a group before the race. Although they need one another, each is entirely devoted to winning. At the end only one person will matter. The rest, even bronze and silver medalists, are the story of who came next. There is great comfort in having come so far, and there will be the same satisfaction merely in finishing, simply in having participated in an Olympic marathon; but for those who feel themselves favored contenders, the strain is apparent.

The world waits, enduring advertisements and the wearying, almost obscene voices of cheerful sports commentators who try to inject human drama into the event. It would be better to let the cameras follow silently, allowing the quiet to convey to viewers the terrible intensity that drives the marathoners forward. Who understands an Olympic marathon anyway? As Joe Henderson, a columnist for *Runner's World*, suggests, "Perhaps a marathon is simply a race with great meaning but no purpose." For many marathoners the significance of the Olympics does not lie in their feelings of patriotism but rather in the long-awaited fulfillment of a personal dream. A year and a half after Montreal, Don Kardong, twenty-nine, former elementary schoolteacher from Spokane, Washington, mused: "I guess everyone, for good and bad reasons, wants to make you their representative. You're wearing the jersey and goddamnit, that's where I'm from, I'm from the United States, and there's my man! And yet you have this feeling like . . . I worked for four years to be here. This is my race. I'm Don Kardong. Yet I understand why they do that. But I saw that kind of pressure destroy a lot of the athletes in terms of their own race."

The marathon bursts free from the Olympic site, away from the confines of the track, playing fields, pools, wrestling mats, closed rooms, static parameters, and the staring eyes. The marathon is run on the road. It takes, in modern times, about 130 minutes before they begin to return one by one, exhausted, like wind-blown leaves. The marathon seizes attention because the word resonates with associations, however clichéd or trivial: Philippides running from the battlefield of Marathon to Athens, gasping out his message and then dying; the first Olympic games in 1896 when a Greek named Spiridon Loues won and ran over the finish line escorted by two crown princes; the Italian Pietri, dazed-looking, staggering, having reached the limit of his capacity, being helped over the line by officials in the 1908 Games, a gesture of compassion that caused him to forfeit his victory; iron-hearted Bikila of Ethiopia running barefoot, at night, in his first Olympics, in Rome, to win the gold medal in 1960. This cluster of images is fascinating and awesome, even to those who don't really know any more about a marathon than the little they glimpse in photos, on TV, or on the streets of Boston.

This special race is the subject of this book's inquiry: what composes the shifting, not totally definable elements of an effort at sustained speed over an arbitrary distance, powered by your own will, your own body's fire. The heroes at the top know how much not only luck but deep perseverance accounts for their success. They were not necessarily the most talented, but they resisted other temptations, other choices; they happened to stick with it; only recently has marathon participation become truly democratic. No longer the reserve of America's private sporting clubs, marathoning now attracts people of every kind and from every walk of life—including children, the crippled, the blind—and they have dramatically changed the sport. They, too, now watch the Olympics every four years. Rich Langsam, from New York City, who would identify himself first as a 2:36 marathoner and second as an assistant comptroller for a midtown firm, was on a date the afternoon of July 31, 1976. "I promised her to barbecue the steak but only when commercials were on," he said. "She was really annoyed that I didn't pay more attention to her or the meal, but I wasn't kidding. It was just one thing nothing was going to keep me from seeing."

The marathon is a game, and it doesn't demean it in any way to insist on this point. A game is played by rules that everyone accepts. One such rule in a marathon concerns the distance: it is an arbitrary rule that will probably continue forever—26 miles, 385 yards, or 42.195 kilometers. The distance, originally chosen as a 40-kilometer course approximating Philippides' run, wavered back and forth several kilometers in distance until the 26.219-mile course first used in the 1908 London Olympics was settled on in 1936 as the standard marathon distance. And why that particular distance? So that the children of the Royal Family could see the start at Windsor Castle (the run finished in front of the Royal Box in White City Stadium). It takes about half an hour to drive a marathon on a highway, about 7 hours to walk it at a brisk pace. But how can one say what 26¼ miles *feels* like? Basically, it feels long, substantially long. Even as a relaxed training run, it takes most runners, even highly trained ones, to the frontiers of discomfort. Distances of that nature are reserved by most runners for that grand classic, the Sunday run. That irreducible space takes time to negotiate. The distance itself is neutral. It happens to be there. Ted Corbitt, one of America's foremost running veterans and an authority on such things as course measurement, has helped work out the strict guidelines now used as the standard for finding the truest representation of an accurate distance. Nothing about a marathon is easy! Ted's packet of guidelines includes precise details on such accepted methods of calibration as surveyor's wheels and bicycle odometers. Certain subtleties must be understood, to wit: a hot day will cause bicycle tires to expand a fractional amount, which in thousands of revolutions over a marathon course can cause the placement of the finish stripe to be misplaced. There is no such thing as a perfectly measured course; the highest standards can only bring one within a plus or minus range of 65 yards, a not unappreciable featherweight of distance to negotiate when one considers how many remember their best marathon time down to the tenth of a second. So every course differs in length, however slightly, as well as in terrain and weather. The hotter the day and the hillier the course, the slower the times. One rule is even simpler in a way than those of determining distance: finish it! And for most, the goal reads: finish it as fast as you can! These marathon artists base their lives on rules even children can understand.

After the 10,000-meter run, the next longest running event in the Olympics is the marathon. The Olympic connection has helped endow the marathon with prestige. People say, "I'm a marathoner" or "I run marathons" with the certainty of someone assured of his position or class in life. They don't say, "I'm a fifteen-mile man" or "a twenty-mile woman." They may have the less impressive choice of saying, "I'm a middle-distance person," but there is no particular distance between 10,000 and 42,195 meters that is more impressive. In fact, the best 10,000-meter runners have moved up in recent years to become the dominant figures in the marathon. They have the leg speed for the shorter track races and enough miles behind them to make an increase in training for the marathon not too difficult. American runners such as Frank Shorter, Kenny Moore, Don Kardong, and Garry Bjorklund all have been or continue to be specialists in running both distances.

But there is a final set of reasons that make the marathon an especially difficult opponent to come up against. There is a particularly perverse quality about 26-plus miles. It cannot be raced the way 20 miles or 50 miles would be. Twenty miles can be run with a hard effort, throttling the whole way, and somehow it rounds off neatly just below the category of an exhausting effort. But the extra 6 miles just cannot be run as hard as the first 20 without somehow taking enough extra punishment to feel thoroughly battered. It is a very long race but an erosive one because the pressure is on pretty much the whole way. A race of 50 miles simply has to be eased into more gradually; the later brutality of the closing effort is expected but delayed for a long time. In a marathon loss of concentration, loss of form, and loss of intensity are problems for almost everyone at the end. There are always late-blooming runners who have husbanded their energies enough to blitz through the fatigued frontline troops, but even these types usually ache and struggle. If it is run at maximum effort, no matter whether one's strategy is run-in-front or come-from-behind, the marathon leaves everyone hobbled ten minutes after stopping. The next morning's run finds them prematurely aged, and a 2-mile jog requires a fair mental effort to get through. Negotiating street curbs and stairs requires crablike locomotion. The physiological payment is heavy: blisters; sore tendons; aching feet; pains in the diaphragm; stitches; the

The start of the New York City Marathon.

fatigue that makes one's arms, shoulders, and eyes feel filled with heavy water; a cranium coated with carbon deposits after unrelentingly burning brain food for so many weeks and months and for the few hours of the race. After the joy of the finish the everyday world, gray by contrast, comes back to claim its due. Hours of free time, normally filled by training runs, confront the weary heroes. Thoughts turn to the next race.

In a way the marathon's appeal is reinforced because the uncertainty is always there: can the distance be completed, can all the potential hazards be avoided?

Everyone seeks control of the event and a mastery of its subtleties. The best marathoners frequently refer to their work as a craft.

They become sensitive to all nuances. The most dramatic example of this comes in races where a misjudged pace, even if amounting to a difference of a few seconds per mile, can be costly later on. Dedicated marathoners have a vision of what they might be. Like artists, they work in lonely isolation, since no one else can run their miles for them. "I've put in my work," they say, "now I'm ready to cash in." But what separates out levels of runners one from another? It is not enough just to work, just to run mile after mile. Judgment is required: how many miles, how fast, how slow, how hard to run them, how many races to run, what one eats, what one thinks, all make a difference. Everyone is different, so everyone's solution is unique and based on the most accurate intuitions and guesses available. Experience helps, but some runners are perhaps just duller about learning from themselves than others.

"It's like a process of fine tuning," remarks one runner. "It's just not something you can force."

Marathoning is an art. There are no rules or techniques that hold for all situations. One's body today is a little different from yesterday's; so is one's mood, one's energy level, and the world's weather and all the other aspects of life that have to be attended to. Sometimes runners put those last considerations to one side.

The sport has changed a great deal. Being a runner or a marathoner can be a way of life, a vocation for the most highly gifted. In 1974 Bob Giegengack, Frank Shorter's coach at Yale, was genuinely worried about the direction of his former protégé's life. "I said to Frank, 'What are you going to do?' " Giegengack reported. " 'Just be a marathon runner all your life? You've got to settle down and earn your living as a lawyer.' " Shorter's route to the Olympic gold medal in 1972 was wonderful, glorious, but only one aspect of the well-rounded life his coach felt the Yale experience would inculcate as an ideal in its graduates. Would his protégé become a professional jock? Would a bright man like Frank choose a life in which, like a dancer, he would always be just one step ahead of age or a ruptured tendon—and with increasing age would he not have to slow down, yield to younger runners? But the lure is strong; the rewards are fascinating and fun. There is a celebrity status to the leaders in the sport. Shorter was sitting in a store in Cambridge, Massachusetts, in early 1977, his mere presence sufficient to serve as an attraction. As he sat there talking with someone he had just met, a woman interrupted the conversation. "Excuse me, Mr. Shorter," she said, "but I just wanted to tell you that my sons and I saw you on TV at the Olympics. You are a hero to my whole family." Shorter smiled politely and thanked her before returning to his conversation, and his fan went off, ecstatic. The earlier heroes of the sport competed in a simpler and more restricted era. No Erich Segal was in Antwerp in 1932 to run alongside Clarence DeMar with a microphone full of questions to satisfy the TV audience at home. The national greats like Johnny Kelley the Elder or DeMar ran at Boston or Yonkers or at local road races in New England, the early center of road racing and marathoning, and then withdrew. None of them were fledgling capitalists in the business of running. There were few running shoes available and the market for them was relatively small. Marathoners worked long hours and slogged out 70 to 80 miles a week, a level of training that is commonly half of what the best do today, but was considered more than ample at the time.

In the United States, more so than in any other country in the world, marathoning has become a tremendously popular sport. An estimated 10 million people run or jog regularly—twice as many as a few years ago. Between 1969 and 1976 the number of American marathons more than tripled—from 44 to 166. And there were 812 sub-3-hour performances by men in America in 1970 as compared to 3,600 in 1976. Some of the early winners of the Boston marathon hitched their way to the race, one of them riding the freight cars illegally and another sleeping on a pool table in the South End the night before the race. Now that some of the top runners allegedly get money under the table to come to certain races, now that various business interests and politicians and running organizers have all become interested in the promotion of so eminently promotable a sport, marathoning is not as private and

Frank Shorter, two-time medalist in the Olympic marathon, finishes second to Bill Rodgers in the 1976 New York City Marathon.

quiet as it once was. Its glorious eccentricity has become common fare on TV. Popularity means more races, better organized and more crowded, more statistics, and more people sharing the benefits. But one can only hope that mass marketing and mass participation will not spoil the marathon's rugged, private qualities. Running is big business now. The once-Spartan black-and-white pages of *Runner's World,* for years the sole magazine devoted to marathon running, have given way to lush four-color ads placed by big shoe companies. With upbeat promo copy they advise the startled reader how anxiously the welfare of his battered feet is being considered by those who really know what running means, because, as one

Nike ad put it, "We're runners, too." But the shoes, even though they now come in shades as varied as those of tropical fish, are hardly the only items partisans can choose from. Running caps, nite-glo vests, sweatbands, vitamin pills, running shorts that "make you feel nude," digital multifunction stopwatches, a slew of books on how to do it, socks, rain suits, drinking glasses and stationery with running themes, and so on ad nauseam. Running magazines and newspapers have burst into existence as rapidly as toadstools after an April rain. There is an irony here, that commercial interests that care for running only when it is big enough to "matter" now get an easy ride in what has been so impoverished a sport.

Running has become a way of life, and a direct source of income for a fair number of people. Perfectly legitimate. But that, too, is a change. Mike Spino, director of Esalen Sports Center, has conducted workshops in the Bahamas on improving one's running. Some runners open running stores. Others offer clinics. Other runners, like this one, write books. Podiatrists who specialize in sports medicine are besieged by new patients. Movie stars and models flaunt trim rear ends on national magazines as they jog off into never-never land. Running is now clean, trendy, in line with our nationally beloved self-improvement themes. Fashion magazines cluck over its therapeutic aspects. *Today's Jogger* asserts that running will turn one's entire body into a "sex organ." A woman in *New York* magazine chatters about the orgasms she experiences when she runs.

Such things could weary the soul. Except the truth is that running is essentially solitary. Watching runners, one senses whether they care, whether they have been out on the road. If they do care and do run faithfully, then the sport lives and one is at peace.

Runners often hear two familiar questions: why do you run? what do you think about when you run? The answer sometimes is that running is just running. Runners don't necessarily give good answers to such basic questions. No one just runs 26 miles casually. No one just runs a 100-kilometer race in a mechanical frame of mind. No one puts himself through 24 hours of continuous running feeling the same as when he started. No runner makes all the choices for training, gives it such care and attention, and chooses to exclude so much else unless impelled to. No one can ever answer fully. Those who test themselves in races, whether they plod through at the rear or blaze through in front, do experience an intensity that is unlike anything experienced in the rest of their lives. But describing it is difficult. It's hard to say where running comes from, what its actual locus is. Running is so often like a dream, especially in races, where the flow of emotion and sensation seem in later recall to be only fragments of faraway memory.

With practice, running becomes increasingly effortless at times. Mental resistance, body ailments, and weaknesses fade away or

Gary Muhrcke, an accomplished marathoner and ultramarathoner, wins the first annual race up the stairs of the Empire State Building.

become utterly familiar. One is launched, detached from ordinary drag. Dr. Richard Schuster, a podiatrist from Queens, New York, who has treated thousands of runners in the past five years says: "I get a lot of guys in here who run for different reasons. I don't know if it's the most common answer, but one of the most impressive to me is 'I like to see the trees go by.' I can just see them running through a forest and watching the trees go by. . . . Others run because they're ex-alcoholics and this is a tremendous substitute addiction. They can handle it this way. Others run because of the creativeness, the clear-out they get from it. They can write better, they can work better. Dr. George Sheehan is a good example of this. He does all his writing when he runs. Others run to keep their weight down. A lot run to keep their pulse and blood pressure down because they check it all the time. Others run because they're hooked. It's the simplest way to put it. If they stop, they have withdrawal symptoms. I have stevedores come in here and they tell me: 'Doc, when I run, you can spit in my face!' "

One woman who has dated a marathoner and known several others says: "They are the most goal-oriented people I've ever met." The admiration in her tone was mixed with a kind of distaste for such driven characters, as if the compulsiveness to run reflected a psychological affliction as much as anything laudable.

Part of the marathon's appeal is its simplicity—how fast can you run between two points? The time will mean something because many others have run it, and although a "good" or "bad" time is always getting faster relative to what it used to be, there is a consensus as to what your performance means in comparison to others. It would certainly be dull for anyone who could overhear the conversation or thoughts of marathoners. So much buzzing speculation about the possibility of running faster times or longer distances per week. It is a way of judging performance, progress, even one's "goodness" as a runner. Fast times breed admiration from friends, and from oneself. You get better. You rise to the top of the pack, you beat your friends and your rivals and your inferior, softer self from five years ago. Hence you are "better," feel "better." So the

Six thousand runners gather in the spring of 1978 for Bloomingdale's 10,000-meter run in Central Park.

goals get centered in quantification, which can be both good and bad. Park Barner, an ultramarathoner from Enola, Pennsylvania, has a single sheet of paper with monthly and yearly mileage totals written out in fine longhand, the neat margins of the columns making a cool and precise record of his lifetime running. Others measure running in blocks of hours, sometimes down to the minute. Still others round off fractions for their log entries, an impossible task for those who need to calculate runs to a tenth of a mile. Zeros exert a particular fascination. A 69-mile week can be almost intolerable for certain sensibilities who would prefer the security of knowing that it was 70. Ninety-nine miles in a week may obviously have the same training effect as running 100 miles, but the difference in how you feel about yourself can be considerable. Of course, it's absurd. There is a tyranny of numbers that afflicts otherwise sober men and women, who give into a kind of superstitious need to encapsulate in round numbers this fluid experience of running. And saying it, acknowledging it, looking at it from a detached point of view doesn't necessarily ridicule it or diminish the effect and the effectiveness of using magical, arbitrary standards to test oneself by. It is a fascinating way of expressing the dimensions of self. Numbers can be as potent and mystical for a runner as the running itself.

Kenny Moore, two-time Olympic marathoner, is a writer for *Sports Illustrated* magazine. His pieces on running are beautiful miniatures, finely rendered scenes that convey much through indirection and understatement.

Kenny travels a lot and the rambling reporter-runner found the time to be interviewed himself for a change on his way from the posh Dorset Hotel in midtown Manhattan to La Guardia Airport, where he was to catch a flight to West Virginia. He was well dressed that afternoon in clothing he said was unusual for him—a tie, corduroy jacket, and dark pants. Unlike his photographs, in which he sports a Vandyke beard, he is now clean-shaven for the first time in eight years. He has steady blue eyes and a clear gaze. His face and long jaw are constructed of wide, smooth, and imperturbable planes. His humor is laconic, quick, gentle—and sometimes shows a few claws. His voice, especially on the phone, has a good-natured dryness, a kind of nasal sound with a slight countryish drawl. He is tall and has a steady, meticulous air. He has a boyish look—something innocent, still undamaged. How he loved Pre!—Steve Prefontaine, the runner who died a few years ago in a car accident in Eugene, Oregon—it shows in a brief comment. And Kenny enjoys talking about Frank Shorter, accepts him as a natural topic, the way one discusses the weather. He was an undergraduate at the University of Oregon where he was a major

Kenny Moore, one of America's best marathoners, reflects on his craft.

in philosophy; he returned there later to get his MFA in creative writing.

"I was born in Portland and moved to Eugene when I was four. I remember watching the local track meets when I was eleven or twelve. In junior high school I felt that I could run long distances, but even though I ran for the cross-country team for North Eugene High School I was not very good. My first coach was great for a runner who was bad. He emphasized getting the most out of it for yourself. So when the competitive aspects became important I could take them in stride. I haven't had a lot of mood swings from being injured or being too tied to winning or losing.

"When I got to the University of Oregon, I had absolutely no trouble adjusting to the coach, Bill Bowerman—sometimes he was irascible and sometimes he was funny and erudite and sometimes profane. I had a marvelous four years with him, and he was astonished at my progress during my sophomore year. I just improved by leaps and bounds. I'd come down from 9:15 to 8:48 for the two miles. A lot of it was hereditary. I was a late bloomer like my father, who grew nine inches after he got out of high school. And a lot of it was Bowerman's genius. I was the kind of runner who didn't thrive on constant hard work. I had to have a lot of easy days.

"Runners run and respond to running in their own way—the essence of it is that it's an individual sport. All the great diversity of the human experience comes into play there. The things I think about while running may simply be of no importance to anybody else. Medical scientists are finding out more and more about how different we are—Rh factors, pigment, mitochondria, levels of enzyme production. It's sort of hackneyed to say that no two human beings are alike, but that's true in practically everything. And then when you throw in the environmental mix, that differentiates people even further. Like George Sheehan says when you're finding yourself and discovering what you're truly meant to be, there are so many forms.

"We are finite and to work for a number of years to try to run

A scene from the Mount Washington road race, 8 miles up to the clouds.

the Olympic marathon and to have it over in a little while and to wake up the next morning as Frank and I did and kind of be depressed and just say let's take a run. . . . Depressed with the fleeting nature, the transient nature of everything. It's funny though. Sprinters talk about how long it takes to sprint. Distance runners say it takes only about forty-five minutes to run a marathon, and if you're running *really* well, it takes less.

"I think this is necessary to get the most out of yourself: that you not care so desperately about success or failure but that you care about doing the thing itself, simply, well. I think of running as a craft, and a good runner as a good craftsman. A lot of runners in the United States are extraordinarily talented, much more talented than I, maybe more than Frank, but they have never done very well. They've performed erratically. They tend to do their worst in things like Olympic trials where Frank and I tend to do our best. They're so desperate for success that their need overcomes the rational faculty that's necessary for success. In a big race, they're so emotional that they just can't go through the proper motions of marathon running, which means starting in a modest frame of mind and pacing yourself, emotionally as well as physically. I've always been impressed by the kind of control Frank has over himself emotionally. And that I think is an underlying characteristic of all good runners. Ron Hill, a runner I respect enormously, lost control of this when he was in the best shape of his life in Munich. He was up at the front and he ran too fast. It was like he was high on something the first six miles. I think some of this was in response to the terrorists, but it was something that neither he nor any of us can really explain. He finished sixth when he might easily have won. I've never talked with him about it. It's just my own observation.

"When you look back at all your best races, nobody runs perfectly all the time. Your best races come—mine did and Frank's did—when we went out with a little bit of doubt, but not desperation, and a little bit of self-confidence, but no vicious commitment to winning. Then you get into it and it turns out you can really rip it. You know, you could ask a question of the first five guys in a pack with ten miles to go and you could pick the winner just by asking them what they were thinking about. Guys who were tense and who might shout 'Go away!'—they would lose. Guys who wouldn't be in a bad frame of mind at all would be much better off. That's bad in a way because it goes counter to the usual stuff about dedication and desire. People who want it the most can't have it because they want it so much. It's Catch 22.

"On the next to last page of *The Sun Also Rises*, Hemingway said: 'If you talk about it, you lose it.' My attention was directed to that by Steve Williams, a sprinter with a marvelous intellect. Steve thought that other sprinters like Houston McTear were marvelous animals, free of intellectualizing. Not that they weren't capable of it but that it didn't enter into their relationship with sprinting. They were at an advantage when they sprinted against Steve, who liked to think about things. There was always that chance in that split second that you'd be thinking instead of acting. Camus emphasizes in *The Myth of Sisyphus* that the difference between pushing that stone up and walking down afterward is all the difference there is between action and contemplation, between thinking and doing. The rock was so heavy that Sisyphus couldn't get it up there unless he put into it everything he had, heart and soul, all his might, so that there was no possibility of thinking. The only time he had for reflection, his true punishment, was on the interminable walk down. All we ever do is act and contemplate. We don't do them at the same time. We flash back and forth really fast, but when you're acting you shouldn't be thinking. The kinds of things you're concentrating on in a marathon when you're running your best are all 'action-thoughts' even though you're thinking: what are other people's tactics going to be, how is your time, what are you going to drink, where is the wind going to hit you the hardest, and so on. That's not thinking—that's doing it. The thinking, the contemplative side, the intellectualizing, runners resist because you run for the running, not to reflect about it later— you do it for the doing. You push the stone, and then if you're lucky or manage to delude yourself into thinking you're not finite, you absolve yourself of having to be intellectually bothered while you're walking down the hill. When you run a good marathon, a hard marathon, it unwinds itself in your mind and you can't sleep after a race—or I can't. It's just like a newsreel that will run itself through two-and-a-half times and there's nothing that I can do except stay up and watch it! So I think it's really understandable that people who are extraordinarily capable and intellectual like Shorter would resist dwelling on it that way. That's why George Sheehan is such an exception.* There's not a lot of pop theorizing from serious runners. One reason of course may be that they're too tired, but I think the main reason is that they're men of action.

"I did have a stock line one time. How come you can't understand marathoning if you can understand Horowitz or Baryshnikov—somebody does something as a kid and practices and spends time at it and little by little over time gets to be a Horowitz or a Baryshnikov. I mean it's terrible to compare yourself with them. But the ability to run twenty-six miles at five minutes a mile—somehow people have just written off becoming a physicist or a pianist, but everybody's got a body so everybody can sort of go out and get a sense of pace and figure it out. For me, having played the piano a little bit, it seems impossible to play like Horowitz. And it is! I don't like to be stood in awe of. Athletes do have a common ground: they run, they feel the same, everybody senses that no matter how hard or how fast that guy runs he probably can't run any harder. That's not true, by the way. Some people can run a lot harder. Pre could run harder than anybody on the earth.

"Runners used to be people who joined absolutely nothing, not even the Road Runners Club. You would have to dun them for their dues and everything. They were all independent, and they would band together out of that independence. Now it's not that

---

* Dr. George Sheehan, marathoner and author of two books on running. See Selected Readings list.

Eugene, Oregon, is the running capital of America. Many fine runners have had their best and most disappointing moments on this track. The 1976 Olympic marathon trials began and ended here.

Warming up before a road race (1976). The outstretched leg belongs to Jacques D'Amboise.

way anymore. Mass participation means a lot of real organizers are coming into this thing. Frank is as independent as they come compared to some of the less independent you read so much about who have this sort of party line about nutrition. Frank is a junk food addict. As for these symposia that I go to every once in a while with people who really care and study physiology, work loads, etc.—Frank doesn't pay attention to that. Frank runs to run and to get the most out of himself. It's not instinctive; it's a honed, intellectual self-analysis. I will tend to fight with a lot of other people, even good runners, because they get caught up in the mileage syndrome. I will recommend more easy days, say, than they would take. It's not because I think for sure it will work but because they've never experimented. Once I said something like that to Frank. He is committed to running a lot and it helps him. He talks about himself as being a compulsive runner. He is not compulsive to the point where he can't make those judgments about getting fit and what's too much and what's not enough. You have to go around to other people recommending that they *not* do what another runner does rather than telling them what they should do.

"I think I'll take a crack at the Olympic trials in '80. I kinda have promised the magazine to go to Moscow anyway and if there's anything I'd rather avoid, it's going to the Olympics as a reporter. I still know which side of the fence I'm on."

2

Body under Stress

Although this section is about what happens to the human body under the stress of running, the very use of the word *stress* has a somewhat harsh connotation. *Stress* brings to mind corrosion and erosion. Stress is to be resisted, eliminated, and avoided, as if running or anything else should be easy, peaceful, and free. The physical stress of running, however, within a variety of individual limits, develops and redevelops the vigor available for more running. The body learns to respond as efficiently and effectively as it can to the demands of such a special work load. For some, running *is* a corrosive element. They either acquire or discover weak points in their mental or physical system and can do no more than a minimal amount of running. Nevertheless, man is meant to be active. The worst stress of all is inaction. Although there is a great deal not known about the physical ramifications of running, many of the basic processes are now clear.

The heart beats more strongly and less often, lung capacity increases, and muscles and tendons grow thicker and more resilient. Metabolic activities learn to smooth the dynamic flow from rest into activity and back into rest again so that one gains, whether running or not running, a sense of "being in shape."

It is not all good news. The marathoner, as he is often reminded by podiatrists, is doing something "unnatural" in running more than 30 miles a week. The body, they say, was not designed to take the pounding of 100 to 200 miles a week on hard surfaces. Not many can subject their bones and muscles to such unremitting mileage without incurring injuries that require specialized treatment. Since many marathoners are willful people with a yen to succeed, they don't know how to handle themselves while healing. Their philosophy is: more not less; if you're tired, never mind; if you're in pain, then it's mental. When the quiet signals the body sends out—soreness, chronic low-grade pain, insomnia, irritability, and others—are ignored, then the body may just give out. Runners' troubles can include back pain, cracks in the pelvic bone, stress fractures in the toes, sciatica, painful knees, an irritable gastric tract, stone bruises, and various other strains that occur mostly to the delicate musculoskeletal system. But everyone's limit is different. The reasons for bodily breakdown are varied and not always completely understood. Only recently have runners benefited from the appearance of a cadre of concerned medical men, particularly podiatrists, who have helped immensely in the prevention and treatment of running-incurred injuries. Horror stories abound of the useless and expensive treatments distance runners have endured when all they needed, for example, was for someone to notice that one leg was slightly longer than the other. The simpleminded days of cortisone injections and rest are gone for good.

When the body runs, it burns fuel. That energy comes mainly from fat and carbohydrates. When a muscle in the leg is stimulated by a nerve impulse, a chemical compound called adenosine triphosphate (ATP) transforms itself into adenosine diphosphate (ADP). ATP is a high-energy molecule basic to cell functioning.

When ATP changes over to ADP, it releases energy that is used in the contraction of muscle fibers. There are a variety of muscle fiber types. In fact, the relationship between two of them has a direct bearing on one's potential for sprint or endurance running. Genetic roulette—what one's parents provided—determines the particular mix of "slow twitch" and "fast twitch" fibers, the "slow" and "fast" referring to the length of time it takes for the muscles to contract. For the endurance athlete a high proportion of slow twitch fibers is best since they fatigue less rapidly than fast twitch fibers. Fast twitch fibers provide speed, but they have fewer stores of energy available to them, and hence can carry on work only for a short period. Research done so far shows that training cannot change the ratio of fast and slow twitch muscles.

Since the time of the Greeks, athletes have favored eating meat before a race. It is only in the last five years, particularly among endurance runners, that the trend has been reversed. Potatoes, pasta, and pancakes are common fare for a runner the day before or even the morning before the race. Protein, although useful for cellular maintenance, is not used as an energy source except when the body is in a fasting or malnourished state. Although the figure cited varies, most people can probably do very well eating 2 to 3 ounces of high-quality protein a day, whether vegetable or animal in origin. Anything consumed in excess of what the body needs not only requires more caloric energy to process, but the excess protein is passed out of the body in the urine as urea. Carbohydrates are available to the body for work from glycogen deposits in the liver and the muscles. (Blood glucose plays a minimal direct role.) Free fatty acids, which the body also uses to provide energy, are made available to the muscles through the bloodstream. The ratio of fat to carbohydrate consumption depends on a variety of factors including how long one is racing, how continuously, how hard, how much previous training is involved, and whether one's diet has been rich in carbohydrates.

It is here that the "maximal oxygen uptake" of a runner—his ability to supply his working tissues with oxygen—determines the choice of fuel. When oxygen is not available to working muscles in sufficient amounts to cover their needs, the body goes into oxygen debt, shifting to anaerobic metabolism. Since fats require oxygen if they are to be burned as fuel, in an anaerobic state (sprinting all-out, for example) the body burns carbohydrates until the subsequent buildup of lactic acid greatly reduces the ability of the muscles to function. In short, one feels tired and has to slow down. The more highly trained a runner is and the greater his maximal oxygen uptake, the more fats contribute to the amount of energy he burns. During aerobic work such as long-distance running, a runner is constantly paying off his oxygen debt and maintaining his ability to move forward, although exhaustion at some finite point will eventually set in.

The problem, from a runner's viewpoint, is that one's store of fuel is finite. One solution is to employ "carbohydrate loading," a procedure that can triple or quadruple the amount of stored glycogen in the muscles. The extra glycogen does not give extra speed, but it apparently lengthens the amount of time one can continue running before reaching exhaustion. Scandinavian researchers have found that it is possible to temporarily supersaturate the muscles with glycogen by manipulating diet and exercise. What runners call carbo loading has been in vogue in the United States since about 1973. One week prior to the marathon the runner depletes his glycogen stores by running for 2 to 3 hours, covering about 18 miles or more. For the next three and a half days carbohydrate intake is kept to a minimum. Essentially only protein is consumed. Any kind of lean meat, eggs, cheese, water, unsweetened tea—that is the usual diet, although a minimal amount of carbohydrate intake helps keep the nervous system functioning efficiently. The effects vary, but some runners find it quite difficult to go through several days of even moderate workouts with muscles that feel near a state of exhaustion. The body, out of necessity, increases the percentage of fat burned. Commonly runners get irritable and tire easily during this period. The breath may smell bad. And it is hard not to eat normally when everyone else around does. Then for the last three and a half days meals consist primarily of carbohydrates and minimal running. The idea is to eat normally, not to stuff oneself. It is also important to drink a lot of water, since glycogen molecules must bind with H_2O to be stored in muscle tissue. In theory, one steps to the line on Sunday noon in a temporary state of glycogen supersaturation. Actual body weight may be a few pounds heavier than normal, but during the course of the run, the extra weight is soon lost.

People react differently to carbo loading. Some swear by it; others have had bad experiences. Individual body variations may change the time needed to reach the peak of glycogen loading after beginning the high-carbohydrate phase of the diet. It may vary from 48 to 72 hours. Since the loading effect lasts only a matter of hours at its peak, timing can be crucial. Lowered resistance to infection and increased susceptibility to injury through fatigue make carbo loading something that should be embarked on thoughtfully. The body is stressed to a high degree, and it is hard to feel completely sanguine about hordes of marathoners going on the diet without knowing, for example, the extreme danger involved in drinking alcohol during the first half of the diet. There are less drastic variations of carbo loading, one of which is to simply take a longish run three or four days before the event and then eat meals high in carbohydrates for a more limited but less strenuously achieved effect.

Disappointing as it is for those seeking rapid improvement through shortcuts, the nutritional experts generally agree that a well-balanced diet should provide everything a marathoner needs. The only advice they offer is that it may be easier for the system to adjust to more frequent, smaller meals. This isn't to say that many marathoners don't swear by such extras to their diet as dolomite, brewers' yeast, B vitamins, vitamin C, vitamin E, and desiccated liver. Dr. Joan Ullyot, a California research physiologist and a talented marathoner, claims that vegetarian runners have the healthiest blood analyses of any group, sedentary or nonsedentary. She also asserts that marathoners "can get away with murder in terms of diet." However true that may be, no one as yet can say with any authority what the long-term effects of diet are on an individual in relation to the special stresses of running. Clearly the body has a remarkable ability to adapt to changes in diet. But what is best for it is not so easily determined.

Some of the effects of running are temporary; others are long-lasting. The degree of conditioning achieved depends on the degree and kind of training. During exercise the body builds up excess heat, particularly in hot weather. This heat is passed off by shunting more blood to the body's surface. The heartbeat increases and each stroke sends out more blood. The heart rate, especially during intense bursts of running, may reach its maximal stroke rate, a level that varies between the sexes (men's hearts have a higher rate) and decreases with age. A typical ten-year-old boy or girl has a maximal heart rate of 210 beats per minute; a twenty-five-year-old a rate of 195; and a fifty-year-old a rate of 175. The flow of blood to the working muscles increases and blood is taken away from less critical areas like the gut. One of the reasons for not running immediately after a meal—though it certainly can be done—is that the competition between the intestinal tract and the leg muscles for adequate blood supply puts a strain on the organism. One of the long-term effects noticeable in highly trained athletes is an increase in the buildup of the capillary network that surrounds the muscles, a factor that enables the oxygen transport system to function more efficiently. Other long-term effects include a slow heartbeat rate at rest and an increased stroke volume, that is, an increase in the amount of blood pumped by each beat of the heart.

The well-trained heart of a marathoner shows definite "abnormalities" on EKG examinations. In fact, these abnormal readings can be a sign of good health, but in the recent past some runners have been prescribed bed rest for their "sick condition." Not only do runners have lower blood pressure than sedentary people, but they have larger coronary arteries as well. Trained runners have extremely favorable concentrations of high-density lipoproteins in the blood, the substances that remove cholesterol from the tissues.

At the top of Heartbreak Hill on the Boston course a runner gets a much-needed douse of cold water. On hot days a runner's rectal temperature can go as high as 105 degrees.

In spite of popular myths about "freezing your lungs" by running in cold weather, most people live in areas where it never gets so cold that there is any danger from breathing freezing air. Whether one runs in the tropics or in Arctic regions, the air is heated to body temperature before it reaches the lungs. Extreme temperatures can create problems, however. When one runs in air cooled to 10° F or below, the wind-chill factor can mean increased danger from frostbite. Similarly, running in the heat presents very real hazards and probably more difficult ones to adjust to. Dr. David Costill, a research physiologist, reported that the top ten marathoners at the 1968 Olympic trials lost on the average over 9 pounds of body weight. Since the body's thirst signals are not

Julie Shea fell victim to the heat and humidity after she finished the Mini Marathon in New York.

necessarily reliable indicators of fluid need, and given the awkwardness of drinking on the run, fluid replacement in hot weather running becomes critical. Most runners not only fail to drink as much as they might during a race but run the risk during the summer of chronic dehydration. Even after races as short as 6 miles, rectal temperatures of over 105° F are not uncommon. On hot days with high levels of humidity, ill-prepared or unacclimatized runners can court heatstroke and kidney failure.

Although Johnny Hayes, the American who won the 1908 Olympic marathon, proudly announced that his training included smoking "only in moderation," the knowledge of how much smoking interferes with exercise is now indisputable. There are a few runners who do manage to smoke heavily and run well for the marathon, but they are simply making it harder for themselves. The respiratory tract must work harder to expel contaminants, and the air passages narrow, thereby increasing the resistance to air movement. Smoke, to mention the most significant of a spectrum of toxins, contains carbon monoxide, which binds with the hemoglobin in the red blood cells, reducing their capacity to carry oxygen to the muscles. Blood pressure and heartbeat rise even higher. Psychomotor abilities deteriorate. And the effects are long-term, since it can take hours for the body to rid itself of carbon monoxide. Unfortunately, for nonsmokers, breathing smoky air, so-called secondhand smoke, is as toxic as inhaling the cigarette smoke directly, although the intensity of its effects depends on the amount of smoke in the air and the amount of time one breathes it. City and suburban runners breathe air heavily polluted by cars, and there is no question that a lot of pollutants enter the lungs. The American Lung Association says that wearing filter masks can remove only the larger particulate matter. The only reasonable choice is to avoid heavily traveled roadways, or to stay out of the mainstream of traffic as much as possible. Perhaps Dr. George Sheehan's wry thought that running in midtown New York is equivalent to altitude training will give some solace. Unfortunately, little is known about the long-term effects of such exposure, and it is ironic that the benefits of running are to some degree undermined by the damage caused by breathing such air. No wonder some people say running will increase the quality of life, not necessarily the quantity.

One of the men most responsible for a revolutionary change in approach toward treating runners is Dr. Richard Schuster, who treated his first runner about five years ago. Thousands have been to see him since. Dr. Schuster developed the use of foot inserts, called orthotics, to handle a variety of imbalance problems found in the feet and legs. Most people can walk or run a little bit without pain. But depending on the severity of "imbalance," the amount and kind of running one does, and one's age and sex, problems of a staggering variety can emerge. The pain can shift in location anywhere from the toes to the buttocks and lower back. The bones and muscles can be affected. The pain can be intermittent and mild or agonizing and continuous. Since runners commonly have over-developed muscles at the backs of their legs that overpower the relatively weaker leg muscles in front, the situation may be further complicated, not to mention the all-too-frequent stiffness and lack of flexibility runners also show. Tight muscles often aggravate any existing predisposition toward trouble. It all serves as a reminder that the body is based on the subtlest interconnections; a fraction of an inch of misalignment may throw off one's entire gait.

Podiatrists deal with a variety of complaints and conditions including abnormal tilting of the front and back of the feet, overstress of the fibrous fatbed under the heel, ligament and tendon strains, stress fractures, impact shock, metatarsal pains, knee pains, Morton's toe (an abnormally short "big toe" forcing the second toe to do the work of the big one), leg length discrepancies, and excess bowing in or out of the leg bones. Treatment may range from a simple heel lift to the use of orthotics, which can compensate for some of the imbalances found. Podiatrists may simply suggest that one do more stretching and strengthening of anterior leg muscles or that one avoid always running on the same side of the road, since the sloped camber of the ground may aggravate a particular imbalance. Although miracles can be worked for many marathoners, others find that injuries are always going to be a problem. In running, the stress absorbed by each foot upon impact of the heel with the ground is three times the stress received in walking. Multiply that by 900 foot strikes a mile over a hard and perhaps rough surface and the reasons for continued trouble become more understandable, if not more acceptable.

One modern introduction to training techniques has been running at altitude, usually between 5,000 and 10,000 feet above sea level. Frank Shorter, two-time Olympic marathoner, has been a great believer in its usefulness. The lack of oxygen at high altitudes forces the body to adjust by an increase in breathing and heart rate. Otherwise, the dangers and the benefits remain controversial at present. Although its proponents claim that it increases the efficiency of the oxygen transport system, researchers like Per-Olof Åstrand and Kaare Rodahl, authors of *Textbook of Work Physiology*, find at present conflicting or uncertain evidence on the benefits of altitude training.

One area where more research needs to be done concerns differences between the sexes. Women have different bodies from men. Dr. Schuster calls them literally softer people. He points out that they have less fibrous tissue, are more flexible, have a greater range of motion and are more susceptible to pains associated with impact shock. Studies have shown that women have smaller hearts, lungs, and bones and less muscle than men. They are also more prone to chronic iron-deficiency anemia, which affects the oxygen-carrying capacity of the blood. Women do have a larger proportion of fat in relation to total body weight, which some argue is an advantage. Dr. Ullyot notes that since female bone structure is lighter and fat weighs less than muscle "a woman usually will weigh less than a man of the same height, and also will have less power to propel the same mass. It is for this reason that the women's mile record will never equal the men's." Dr. Ullyot goes on to cite Dr. Ernst van Aaken, a German running coach, biochemist, and longtime booster of women's distance running abilities.

Dr. van Aaken theorizes that women have a distinct advantage in long-distance endurance events because, Ullyot notes, "much of the body's fat—especially that stored by trained long-distance runners—is highly active metabolically and serves as a superior fuel for endurance performance." Women also are able to run, within individual limits of comfort, during menstruation and throughout pregnancy.

It is abundantly clear from examining the origins of distance running in Britain in the late nineteenth and early twentieth centuries, that training strategies were based on a flimsy knowledge of physiology. The growth of modern training techniques has been slow. In Britain—the fatherland of modern distance running—runners sometimes endured removal of their spleen as a cure for shortness of breath. In his book, *Modern Distance Running*, Antony Ward mentions some of the rough home remedies employed by pedestrians, as professional runners and walkers were once called. They used emetics, violent purgatives, forced sweatings, venesectomies (opening of the veins for bloodlettings), ate large amounts of almost raw meat and dry stale bread, no vegetables, and took in a minimum of liquid. The "gentlemen amateurs" who were drawn to running in the nineteenth century simply adopted these measures with what must have been occasionally dubious results. Certainly there was no heavy training for marathons in the early years, either in terms of miles covered or days per week of running. Such essentially casual training makes the times of the past merit respect. The effort was always difficult, the motivation always intense, and runners simply tried their hardest within limitations that changed quite slowly.

Testimony about the world of training in the 1920s and 1930s in the United States comes from Glasgow-born Jock Semple. Known to the world as the resident guru of the Boston Marathon, he operates out of his tiny physiotherapy office in the Boston Garden. Jock, whose running career began in 1918 with the Clydesdale Harriers, a running club in Scotland, emigrated to Philadelphia in 1923. Semple ran his first marathon in 1926 on the roads from

Valley Forge to Philadelphia. He was a good runner in his day. He held the course record of 2:39 on the Pawtucket, Rhode Island, marathon, which he won twice, and he was frequently among the top finishers at Boston.

"I used to train eighty, ninety miles a week in the 1920s," Jock said. "I used to run only Tuesday, Thursday, and Sunday. On Sunday I would take a long walk or a long run. It was a lot tougher to train because you worked harder and more hours in the week. Spaulding made a training shoe for runners—there were no custom-made shoes available—but it was too narrow for guys with wide feet. Still you took what you got. You taped your feet up and got blisters and bloodied shoes. And training sneakers cost ten dollars a pair, which was a lot of money then. They had leather or special kangaroo uppers. Eventually crepe rubber bottoms came in, but the shoes were very heavy.

"Most fellows were great believers in a steak three or four hours before the race. I did a lot of experimentation on my own. I tried eating a big steak the night before. Once I ran a race in Manchester after a breakfast of two grapefruits and I won the race. But usually I'd have a bowl of oatmeal and honey. It was considered taboo to take water during a long run so even on the hottest days we went without. Of course salt pills and drinks like ERG were unknown. There was an old guy from Canada who used to put a green cabbage leaf on his head under a handkerchief to ward off the sun. Then a few runners began to use handkerchiefs tied with a knot in each corner for the hot days. The treatment for a groin pull was to stand in a shower under hot and cold water. Or you'd bathe an injury in Epsom salts.

"There wasn't much interest in marathoners. We'd run for miles in a race and hardly see a dozen people out to watch us. We ran from Laurel (Maryland) to Baltimore one day in a race and this man was leaning against a wall facing away from the road. He couldn't even be bothered to turn his head! We were considered the freaks of the athletic world. What the hell you want to run twenty-six miles for? they'd ask. How much you get? Everything was measured in terms of money. In those days college guys wouldn't dream of running marathons. There was a track coach at Boston College who used to say anything over two miles was crazy. The public had their pet things to say, too. 'What are you running for? President?' Or they'd say, 'Where's the fire?' I couldn't practice walking because I got enough ridicule for running as it was."

The 1930s and 1940s were a time when various training methods were developed by various star coaches and star runners. Some of the ideas were genuinely new. Others, as Ted Corbitt once pointed out, needed to be rediscovered before making an impact. And sometimes certain ways of running were used in practice by runners who never referred to them with the terms current now. One of the perpetual themes is to find a balance between moderate and fast running. Too much moderate or slow running doesn't seem to develop a marathoner's ability to the fast edge he may be capable of. Too much fast running runs the risk of physical injuries or mental staleness, though the latter is also apparent sometimes in slow running. There are a number of complicating factors that have been present in this intense search for bettering one's speed. There is the matter of individual variation in body and temperament—and native talent. Just as important is training background—how long one has been running. It may be all right for Emil Zatopek to bash out prior to his 1952 Olympic marathon, on a daily basis, 20 fast intervals of 200 meters, 40 fast intervals of 400 meters, and another 20 fast intervals of 200 meters (a slow 200-meter jog followed each fast interval). But there is a danger in blindly copying a schedule, rather than adapting a general principle to one's individual capacities. Sometimes the inspiration of an athlete's example can be potent. Gordon Pirie, star British middle-distance runner, was mesmerized by Zatopek in the 1948 London Olympics. Pirie, like Zatopek, had fierce dedication and an appetite for hard training that greatly set him at odds with what he derided as the British-gentlemen-don't-try-so-hard approach. But then how does anyone ever gauge improvement or know that ultimately one system is better than any other? As the history of the sport grows and the stock of books, pamphlets, charts, and ideas increases, a runner has to feel his way along. Since one can never repeat a race to know whether having done it differently would have mattered, it is only one's instinct and judgment that ultimately determine a particular program.

In the 1930s, the Swedish coach Gosta Holmer, stung by Sweden's continual defeat in international running events, became "determined to create something new and something that suited the Swedish mind and the nature of the country." What he called Fartlek, or "speedplay," consists in long running, on the roads or over the countryside, preferably over varied terrain, alternating fast bursts with slower stretches of running. The fast running varies in length according to the day, one's mood, and one's level of energy; one should finish feeling tired but not completely fatigued.

Interval training, which is a series of hard, fast measured runs, usually on a track, with a short rest in between each run, was developed by a German coach named Woldemar Gerschler. As the body enters oxygen debt, the system learns to operate in a state of fatigue. Judicious use of interval training can do wonders for increasing one's speed. But its overuse or misuse can drive a runner into staleness or injury.

Another influential coach has been the late Percy Cerutty, whose Portsea training camp bred such great runners as Herb Elliot and John Landy. Cerutty's approach was to inspire and encourage his athletes to put out a tremendous effort in a demanding environment without the formal lash of the stopwatch. Cerutty, who knew and greatly admired ultra-runner Arthur "Greatheart" Newton, appears in his later photographs, mustachioed and tanned, driving his white-haired supple self over sandhills. His books, like that with the characteristic title *Be Fit! Or Be Damned!*, include advice on raw foods and vitamins, belly breathing, running style, mental attitude, weight training, sandhill running, a preference for "speedplay" as opposed to interval training—these are his major themes. Interval training with its more regimented timed intervals on a track stands in contrast to the looser, more improvisational

The finish of a 1976 6-mile race in Central Park.

nature of speedplay with its varied terrain and irregular bursts of speed. A man with whom Cerutty is often contrasted is Arthur Lydiard of New Zealand, who coached Peter Snell, Murray Halberg, and Barry Magee, all medalists in the 1960 Olympics. Lydiard, outwardly a less flamboyant patriarch, developed a basic system of 100+ miles a week training that adds stamina to basic speed. Lydiard believes in graduated peaking for a race season after developing one's endurance. (Peaking is bringing one's speed and strength to a high point for a particular race or series of races.) His program also includes interval training, uphill and downhill running, and long, fast running near one's aerobic capacity.

Van Aaken has also been an influential figure. He proposes easy running to build endurance and keeping food intake to a minimum to increase the favorable balance between heart capacity and body weight, which results in increased power. He argues that Zatopek's relatively slow interval training was distorted by others who increased the tempo of the fast runs to overly stressful levels, breaking runners down rather than building them up. His ratio of one fast mile for every 20 slower miles is equivalent to what Joe Henderson, a writer for *Runner's World*, popularized as Long Slow Distance (LSD) running.

In spite of the progress made with these sometimes conflicting schools of thought, Fred Wilt, a scholar of training techniques and a once-talented runner himself, says: "Training used by the ancient Greeks was in many ways similar to workout routines now followed by contemporary runners. For example, the principles of 'overload,' gradual adaptation to stress and progressive resistance, are as true today as then."

If runners haven't discovered anything entirely new, as Fred Wilt suggests in his series *How They Train*, then what explains better performances? He suggests that this is due to the increased number of miles run, the greater percentage of training at a faster pace, more frequent workouts, more time spent in workouts, less time off from running, the more precise use of aerobic and anaerobic training, the greater total number of athletes competing, the greater number of races available, and better roads and tracks.

3

Olympics and Olympians

In both the ancient and modern Olympics, glory has gone to the winner. All the rest who merely finish most likely will not be remembered very long. The Greeks, unlike us, were not generous about prizes: there was first place and there was nothing else.

The direct inspiration for the marathon comes from Greek history but pertains to war, not sport. When the Athenians were preparing to repel the Persian invasion in 490 B.C., the Greek generals sent a messenger, a trained runner from a class of men known as hemerodromi, to Sparta for an unsuccessful petition for aid to repel the invasion. The runner's name was probably Philippides, not Pheidippides. The one-way trip between Athens and Sparta over mountainous terrain is about 150 miles and took 1 to 2 days. Although Herodotus does not mention the return trip, that, too, must have taken place shortly after, given the urgency of wartime preparations in Athens. The Persians and Athenians then clashed at the site of Marathon. The victorious Greeks sent a herald to announce victory to the anxious elders in Athens, 24 kilometers distant. The legend attributes the run to the same Philippides and has the messenger die just after gasping out his message. The truth of the incident hardly matters. The legend has been a potent one, and Robert Browning's poem, *Pheidippides*, which he wrote in 1879, helped move the event into the realm of enduring myth.

> *Run, Pheidippides, one race more! the meed is thy due!*
> *"Athens is saved, thank Pan, go shout!" He flung down his*
>   *shield,*
> *Ran like fire once more; and the space 'twixt the Fennel-field*
> *And Athens was stubble again, a field which a fire runs*
>   *through,*
> *Till in he broke: "Rejoice, we conquer!"*
> *Like wine through clay,*
> *Joy in his blood bursting his heart, he died—the bliss!*

The Greeks admired runners who covered immense distances, but the Olympiads of the Greeks in all their quadrennial appearances over a period of almost 1,200 years (776 B.C.–A.D. 393) had as the longest Olympic running race the dolichos. The runners covered 24 lengths of the stadium, with sharp turns around a post at either end to cover a total distance of about 4,600 meters, or about 2¾ miles. The runners went naked and barefoot in their competitions. When the victor in each of the various competitions was crowned, he assumed godlike properties, becoming in a sense the representative of the god. Such a man's fame, honor, and well-being were often ensured for the rest of his life. The games enjoyed immense prestige throughout ancient Hellas, and since the Olympiad was a festival in honor of Zeus, all wars, legal disputes, and death penalties were suspended for the duration of the games. The patron state of the games was Elis, a permanently neutral and sacred territory. As the games approached, heralds went everywhere throughout Hellas to announce the date they would be held. Pilgrims, whether spectators or athletes, had their personal safety guaranteed on their way to and from Olympia. Slaves, women, and foreigners could not compete in the Games. Only those of pure Greek descent were allowed to enter. According to the German scholar, Ludwig Drees, the Olympiads were not designed to promote sport for its own sake or to break records but to promote the Greek ideals of physical perfection and military proficiency.

There were strict rules to ensure that no bribing of judges would be tolerated. Athletes often had trainers and their training regimens included a vegetarian diet. Then, as now, the Olympics were immensely popular, but the crush of noisy crowds and the heat and dust were sometimes appalling. Access to drinking water, for example, was a chronic problem. No married women were permitted to watch the Games under penalty of death with the exception of one of the priestesses. However, at the quadrennial festival of Hera, there was a footrace for girls. They ran with their hair unpinned and wearing knee-length tunics cut to expose their right breasts.

Eventually the Olympiads were banned as a pagan cult by Emperor Theodosius I at the close of the third century A.D. During the nineteenth century, there were a few attempts in Greece and elsewhere to promote Olympic-style games well before Baron Pierre de Coubertin made his formal proposal for the modern Olympiads, but these attempts were not successful. Between 1859 and 1888 there were four "Olympic" games in Athens held in a somewhat chaotic, disorderly fashion, complete with olive wreaths and barking dogs that chased the runners. It was Coubertin's persistence that led to the establishment of the modern Olympics. He was a dedicated French patriot who was appalled by France's humiliating defeat by the Prussians in 1870. He was extremely interested in reforming existing standards of education and placing a rigorous emphasis on sport as a means of revitalizing French youth. He also began to promote international sporting competitions, and his first proposal for Olympic Games came in a lecture at the Sorbonne in 1892. The public was puzzled, indifferent, and only occasionally enthusiastic. Politics, as always, was present even in the early stages. Tension between the Germans and the French was still high and the organizational preparations were fraught with conflicts. In spite of the emphasis on the international character of the Games, the first series in Athens in 1896 was restricted mostly to Europeans and North Americans.

In 1894, as plans for the Olympic Games became more precise, Michel Breal, a French scholar, put up a silver cup as the first prize in a footrace he thought should be called the marathon in honor of Philippides' run.

And so on April 10, 1896, on a hot Sunday afternoon, 25 runners set off on the start of the world's first marathon. The 40-kilometer course went from the bridge at Marathon to the finish line in the Olympic stadium in Athens where 100,000 people were waiting. In the small villages along the road everyone had turned out to watch, especially to cheer the Greek runners. The Greeks had done poorly until then in the Games, and hopes were high that somehow a Greek might win. Although the Games themselves were well run and attracted large crowds, the first Olympics was not truly representative of the best athletes from around the world. And in the case of the marathon race, no one really knew anything about how to prepare for it.

The winner, a twenty-four-year-old Greek named Spiridon Loues, was a peasant from the village of Marousi, which lay about 7 miles from Athens. Loues earned his living as a water carrier who trotted alongside his mule from Marousi to Athens and back, a distance usually totaling about 15 miles. The night before the race he went to church to pray. His training meal the next day included a whole chicken.

The race itself had some classic tactical aspects to it. The early leader did not last. Lemeusieux, a Frenchman, dashed off at a fierce clip, opening up a 3-kilometer lead by the 15-kilometer mark. But by the time he and Flack, a smooth-running Australian, had exchanged the lead a few times, they had both burned themselves out. Poor Lemeusieux, whose coach had been riding a bicycle and accidentally knocked him to the ground, lost his lead shortly after 30 kilometers. An exhausted Flack, who then took the lead, lost it himself a few kilometers later. He collapsed and was taken to Athens in a horse-drawn ambulance. Loues and another Greek ran shoulder to shoulder for a while until they reached the outskirts of Athens, where Loues, "his face twisted with pain," pulled ahead at last. It was a classic tortoise strategy, running an even pace from the start, letting the early leaders go out fast, and then in the latter stages of the race catching up to everyone again. The yelling, the tears, the pandemonium, were tremendous as the Greeks welcomed their native son into the stadium. The two princes, Constantine and George, jogged the final lap on the track with the new hero as dozens of officials ran alongside. Loues crossed the line in 2 hours 55 minutes 20 seconds. The king himself stood and waved his nautical cap in homage to the winner. Loues was showered with gifts and extravagant proposals. A tailor, a barber, and a restaurant owner offered him their services free forever. Two other men offered him handsome sums of money. To all of this Loues simply said no. He apparently did not want to jeopardize his amateur status for future races, although he never won an important race again. The one thing he asked for from his monarch was a cart and horse, "so I won't have to run after my mule anymore."

The development of the marathon was slow, and in spite of a few exceptional annual races, serious interest was generally confined to a few dozen athletes and spectators at the lesser-known events. Road conditions were not good for running and poorly developed training methods were as much a hindrance as a help. Although marathon winners have emerged from the Olympics as worldwide heroes—men like Zatopek, Bikila, Shorter—it is only in the past few years that there has been something equivalent to an explosion of general and sustained interest as well as an understanding of what marathoning involves.

In 1896 America's first marathon was held on a 25-mile course from Stamford, Connecticut, to the Knickerbocker Athletic Club at the Columbia Oval in New York City. The September run took the 30 entrants through mud, slush, and cobbled streets. The winner, John J. McDermott, had a time of 3:25:55. There were 9 other finishers, and the reporter for the *New York Times* described the

The leaders pass through early on during the 1978 Boston Marathon. The eventual winner is Bill Rodgers (wearing number 3).

scene at the finish: "Women who knew only that the first race of its kind ever held in the country was nearing a finish, waved their handkerchiefs and fairly screamed with excitement. Men dashed from their seats and down beside the track to get a look at the Americo-Marathon victor. There was a pandemonium of joy. Judges stopped their work; athletes found time to become spectators."

The "pale-faced" McDermott went on to win America's second marathon in Boston in 1897 in what was to become America's oldest annual marathon. There were only half as many starters as had gathered in Stamford, but from such humble beginnings came one of the most colorful and prestigious international marathons. The date was April 19, now the traditional day the Boston event is held. The runners come in from the countryside west of Boston through the suburbs to finish in the city proper. The start was originally in Ashland, not by Hopkinton Green as it is now, and the finish was at the Irvington Street Oval. The modern race ends in front of the Prudential Center. The course length, like many marathons in the early years, changed frequently. But as in New York, McDermott had about 25 miles to cover. He posted a much-improved time of 2:55:10, although he had to walk three times in the last 10 miles of the race. There were 8 finishers.

In 1900 at Boston a Canadian runner, James Caffrey, turned in a fine winning time of 2:39:44, the first one under the 2:40 barrier. The winning times began to improve steadily, if slowly, with some obvious exceptions like the 97° scorcher in 1909 where Henri Renaud of New Hampshire chugged in with a 2:53:36. Over the years Boston's quirky mid-April weather has subjected runners to snow, rain, and blasting heat.

The Olympic Games continued. The 1900 Paris marathon was held, as so many marathons have been, under the worst conditions for good performances—July 19 was extremely hot. The French organization for the race was spotty. The winner, a former baker's assistant, was French, but nagging doubts clouded his victory. Did the French runners take shortcuts through the maze of Parisian

The crowd in front of the Prudential Center in Boston waits for the winner to appear (1978).

streets? The Americans, when it was their turn, ran the Games under the shadow of the 1904 World's Fair in Saint Louis. European representation in the entire range of events was very poor. The course for the marathon took in seven steep hills and was held on another blistering summer day. The country roads were made more torturous for the runners since the automobiles of attendants and officials spewed thick dust into the air, so much so that the runners were sometimes not visible to motorists who followed behind. Tom Hicks of the Cambridge, Massachusetts, YMCA won over two other talented and experienced American marathoners, Fred Lorz and Arthur Newton, but only after his handlers provided him with strychnine, raw eggs, and brandy. Lorz, who had been staggered by his fast pace in the heat, was driven along the roads by a sympathetic doctor until about 5 miles from the finish, where, revived, he jumped out ahead of the other runners and finished to the cheers of the stadium crowd. He was barred from amateur athletics for life until some friends managed to get him reinstated and he went on to win at Boston the following year. The runner who finished in fourth place in Saint Louis was a Cuban mailman, who ran wearing black trousers cut off at the knees and leather shoes. Along the way he snatched two peaches from some picnickers, climbed an orchard fence to eat some green apples, later lay down until his stomach cramps eased, and still managed to finish creditably.

The 1908 Olympics in London were run over a course from the High Street Gate at Windsor Great Park to the track of the newly constructed White City Stadium at a point directly opposite the Royal Box, a distance that has since become the standard. The finish on that hot July day was remarkably close, and the picture of an exhausted Dorando Pietri being helped over the finish line by officials is one of the classics in the history of sports. Pietri had arrived on the track so thoroughly spent that he turned in the wrong direction. Then he fell to the ground several times while Johnny Hayes, the American favorite, closed to within yards before Dorando was pulled first over the line. Pietri was taken off to the hospital, and although Hayes got the gold medal, Pietri was the sentimental favorite. Queen Alexandra awarded him a duplicate of the American's gold cup. And in America, Irving Berlin wrote a song about Dorando, which was his first popular success.

Hayes and Dorando (as he was popularly known) both turned professional and clashed in several marathon races in the United States. This burst of professional and amateur marathoning amid tremendous popularity lasted from the fall of 1908 through the spring of 1909. It was an early peak of interest. Like the earlier pedestrian races in the 1880s and 1890s, a few were held in the old Garden in New York City on a 10-laps-to-the-mile track. The Garden was packed with spectators, smoke, dust, and yelling. In their first rematch, Dorando must have gotten eminent satisfaction. He beat Hayes by less than a hundred yards. Tom Longboat, an Onondaga Canadian Indian, a 1907 winner at Boston and 1908

Olympic marathoner, took Dorando on twice and beat him each time, undoubtedly making *him* feel better for his failure to finish in London earlier in the year.

A Yonkers race with a field of 150 and a Rye-to-Columbus Circle race with 272 starters were held in the winter and spring of 1909. The last big professional marathon that year was held at the New York Polo Grounds with six great runners: Dorando; Hayes; Longboat; Matthew Maloney (three-time winner of the three marathons he had entered that year); Alfred Shrubb, the great English middle-distance man; and Henri St. Yves, a French waiter running against 40 to 1 odds. In spite of the heavy rain and the soggy footing, St. Yves won by almost five minutes over second-place finisher Dorando. St. Yves's time was 2:40:50.

The 1912 Olympic marathon in Stockholm was won by Kenneth McArthur of South Africa. At the next Games, in 1920 in Antwerp, the Finns began their domination of world-class distance running—a domination that lasted into the mid-1930s. Nineteen-year-old Paavo Nurmi, the "Flying Finn," won a track *and* a cross-country 10,000-meter run at the 1920 Games. His steady pacing and dedicated training, most of which he conducted actually holding a stopwatch, made a tremendous impression on the world of distance racing. His fellow countryman, ace middle-distance runner Hannes Kolehmainen, took the gold in the marathon in 2:32:35, followed by Finns in fifth, ninth, and tenth places. Kolehmainen, however, like every other Olympic gold medalist in the marathon who has tried for a win at Boston, failed in 1917 to place better than fourth there.

The 1924 Olympics in Paris marked the second appearance in the Games of Clarence DeMar, a printer from New Hampshire. He had been twelfth in Stockholm, and he came to Paris as the four-time winner of the Boston Marathon. The Finns, however, continued their domination as Albion Stenroos, aged forty, a woodworker and sewing machine salesman, took the gold. DeMar took third place less than a minute behind an Italian runner. Two years later, Stenroos and DeMar clashed head on at Boston. But a nineteen-year-old runner beat Stenroos by 4 minutes, and DeMar finished about 3 minutes behind the Finn for third. DeMar made his final appearance in the Olympics at the age of thirty-six in the Amsterdam Games of 1928, where he finished twenty-seventh. The winner that year on a flat course in 2:32:57 was El Ouafi, a French Algerian and a former dispatch bearer in the French Army in Morocco. Those Games also marked the first time that women were allowed to compete in track and field events.

Since 1896, the average speed of the marathon had been slowly but consistently picking up from Spiridon Loues's 8.34 mph to 9.33 mph in 1912 and 10.44 mph in 1920. That last improvement came from Kolehmainen's Olympic victory. The Finn's speed stood until 1932 when Norio Senzaki of Japan edged it up to 10.53 mph. Today a runner must average 12 mph to be included in the top handful of record holders.

The 1920s and 1930s saw a number of marathons established around the world that have since become classic events, although many were interrupted for a period by the political turbulence that preceded World War II. The Kosice marathon in Czechoslovakia (1924) had to be suspended for a long period, as did the quadrennial British Commonwealth Games, but both resumed in the postwar period. Others continued uninterrupted. The London Polytechnic Harriers marathon, which is the world's second oldest annual marathon, was simply rerouted as necessary.

The 1932 Los Angeles Olympic marathon was won by Juan Carlos Zabala of Argentina in a record time of 2:31:36. Four years later Zabala tried for a victory again in the Berlin Olympics of 1936. He was caught 7 kilometers after the turnaround that marked the halfway point by Kitei Son, a Korean running under Japanese colors, and Ernest Harper of England, a twenty-nine-year-old English miner. Zabala, devastated, had to let the duo pull away, and he dropped off to the side of the road to sit down at 31 kilometers. He was unable to finish. The short, featherweight Son, whose training had included running with sand in his pants and rocks strapped to his back, eventually pulled away from second-place finisher Harper to set a new Olympic record of 2:29:19.

Also present at the Games was Loues. On opening day, dressed in his peasant garb, he walked across the stadium field to the reviewing stand. There, tears running down his face, he presented Adolf Hitler with a sprig of wild olive from Mount Olympus. Loues said: "I present to you this olive branch as a symbol of love and peace. We hope that the nations will ever meet solely in such peaceful competition." Hitler clasped Loues's hand.

Emil Zatopek, an immensely popular, good-natured Czech middle-distance runner who dabbled spectacularly in the marathon, brought not only interval training to the attention of the world but the effectiveness of tremendous dedication to one's work. This was training on a much higher level than had been seen previously. According to his friend Pirie, Zatopek would jog for hours on the same spot, reading a book or listening to the radio. "Everything was fun. On washday at home he piled all the dirty clothes in the bath and ran on them." He married Dana, a javelin thrower, in 1951, and one winter when she had a broken ankle he ran with her on his back through deep snow. One of their games was to stand facing each other and fling a javelin at each other—hard as they could—catch it and throw it back. Zatopek had no training secrets. He liked intense competition, but at the same time he would startle runners in a track race by patting them on the back and encouraging them to run faster. He ran with a bobbing head and a contorted face, vividly energetic in spite of the surface ungainliness.

In the 1948 Olympics "Emil the Terrible" was the 10,000-meter champion. In 1952 in Helsinki, in the only triple of its kind, he won the 5,000- and 10,000-meter races and the marathon—his first. He said afterward, probably puckishly: "The marathon is a very boring race." Zatopek was held in disfavor by the Czech officials who took control after the democratic thaw in 1968. He lost his coaching job and was assigned to collect garbage in the streets of Prague. When ordinary Czechs came up and helped him in his work, the government assigned him for a while to installing insulation indoors. He now lives in a suburb outside Prague.

One of the most revealing stories about Zatopek comes from Australian Ron Clarke, one of the greatest track racers and a dominant figure throughout the sixties. Clarke himself dabbled several times in "those damn marathons." He ran a personal best of 2:20+ in the 1960 Tokyo Olympics, just five minutes behind the leader. Clarke's great disappointment, and one that so many criticized him for, was winning everything but a gold medal at the Olympics. He and Zatopek struck up a friendship, and in 1966 Clarke visited Czechoslovakia for a race.

"As I was leaving the country, Emil slipped a little parcel into my pocket and said, 'I want you to take this to remember me by because you deserve it.' I thought it was jewelry or some such thing so I thanked him and didn't open it. He was obviously embarrassed giving it to me, and I didn't want to embarrass him further by opening it and thanking him profusely. On the plane, when no one was looking, I pulled out the parcel and opened it— and there was Emil Zatopek's ten-thousand-meter gold medal from 1952. An inscription on it read simply, 'To Ron Clarke, Emil Zatopek; Prague, July 19, 1966.' "

The 1950s saw the brief dominance of Englishman Jim Peters, who was the first marathoner to break the 2:30 barrier. (He ran a 2:29:28 in 1951 at the Polytechnic Harriers' marathon.) He did it an astounding three more times over the next two years before others caught up with him. Riveted by the idea that "the more you put in, the more you take out," the amiable Peters was a hard worker by contemporary standards. He had been a good middle-distance runner, although he was once lapped by Zatopek in the Olympic 10,000 meters. He stumbled into marathon running, not meaning to go too far with it, worried as he got into his thirties that his belly was getting too big. With the support of his wife and his coach, Johnny Johnston, Peters entered his first marathon in 1951. At the end of the race he had become the first Englishman to break the 2½-hour mark. His first world record came a year later when he turned in a time of 2:20:42, at the Polytechnic race from Windsor to Chiswick. He was not aware of doing anything special during the race. His legs ached, he recalled later. He felt like "an awful fool" being out there and vowed that it would be his last race. His main thought was simply to finish. Peters is also remembered for his heartrending loss at the Empire Games at Vancouver in 1954, where he entered the stadium first at the end of a hot day's marathon but collapsed. Disoriented, staggering to his feet and collapsing repeatedly in a manner reminiscent of Dorando's terrible struggle, he was taken off to the hospital as the other finishers ran past him. Later the Royal Family presented him with an award for his gallantry.

The Melbourne Olympic marathon in 1956 saw the close of a long rivalry between two remarkable runners. Alain Mimoun, a Frenchman of peasant origin from a mountain village in Algeria, had been chasing Emil Zatopek in the Olympics in 1948 and 1952. In the 1948 London Games, during the 10,000-meter run, Zatopek flew ahead of the field at the end leaving a 48-second gap between himself and Mimoun, who finished second. In 1952 in Helsinki, Mimoun trailed Zatopek again—in the 5,000-meter event by 8/10ths of a second and in the 10,000-meter event by 15 seconds— taking the silver medal in both races. In 1954 Mimoun's running career ended when sciatica hobbled him. A score of doctors were unable to help. Finally, in desperation, Mimoun, on the advice of a friend, made a pilgrimage to the Basilica of St. Theresa of Lisieux in late 1955. The cure worked and in 1956 he entered the marathon at the age of thirty-six. Hardly anyone—except Zatopek—thought he had a chance to win. But he did win, not looking over his shoulder for his rival until he was on the stadium track at last. This was the only marathon Mimoun ever ran.

The late 1950s and early 1960s saw a continued drop in record times and the emergence of outstanding American and Japanese marathoners. The size of the sport and the numbers of participants were still relatively small. In 1963 Toru Terasawa of Japan ran a world record time of 2:15:15. The first 10 finishers that day all turned in times under 2:20. The Japanese had put a tremendous amount of work into their marathon training in preparation for the 1964 Tokyo Games, and the benefits of this work were apparent for the rest of the decade. At Boston in 1965 Japanese runners took first, second, third, fifth, and sixth slots; in 1966 they took first, second, and third; in 1967 third place and in 1969 a Japanese runner again was first.

The 1960 Rome Olympics marked the emergence of African runners when Abebe Bikila of Ethiopia, running barefoot through the streets, won in 2:15:16 to set—by less than a second—a new world and Olympic marathon record. "The marathon distance is nothing for me," he said. "I could have kept going and gone around the course another time without difficulty." Little specific information has survived about Bikila. He has left a remarkable impression, in film clips, showing his graceful, focused concentration, and his barefoot running. In 1964 at Tokyo, Bikila wore shoes and this time won by more than four minutes over the second man in 2:12:11, another world record. He had improved on his previous Olympic time by more than three minutes. After finishing he did some easy stretching and some knee bends. But in Mexico City in 1968 he missed a third consecutive Olympic gold medal when an injured ankle forced him out of the race, and teammate Mamo Wolde went on to win. A year later in Addis Ababa, Bikila, dazzled by the headlights of an approaching car, overturned in the VW he was driving. The accident left him paralyzed from the waist down. As an honored imperial guard of Emperor Haile Selassie and a national hero, Bikila was flown to England for treatments that were unable to change his condition. Bikila, married and the father of four children, was visited by William Oscar Johnson, a writer for *Sports Illustrated,* several years before his death in 1973. "At home, Bikila is wheeled about by his brother. He speaks in Amharic through an interpreter. There is an almost incandescent intensity about the man; he frowns gravely at each question asked and his long, tapered fingers frequently make nervous sketches in the air as he answers. He is brave and fatalistic and enormously dignified when he speaks of his fate.

" 'Men of success meet with tragedy,' he said softly. 'It was the will of God that I won the Olympics, and it was the will of God that I met with my accident. I was overjoyed when I won the marathon twice. But I accepted those victories as I accept this tragedy. I have no choice. I have to accept both circumstances as facts of life and live happily.' "

In the late 1960s tough-talking Derek Clayton of Australia set two new world's records within two years of each other, one of which still stands at the top of the list. In 1967 on the Fukuoka course the civil engineering draftsman ran 2:09:36, nine minutes better than his previous personal best. In 1969, on an Antwerp course, following a knee operation, he ran a 2:08:33 that is in the books as the fastest marathon ever. There have been unresolved doubts expressed about the accuracy of the course. But in any case the use of the term *world record* in a marathon is somewhat misleading. Weather and terrain make no two marathons exactly alike.

Clayton's training before his retirement was fierce in intensity, volume, and speed. He endured two operations for removal of damaged cartilage in his right knee and for a torn Achilles tendon. He called himself "one of the toughest competitors in the world." He went on to say: "This is why I run, because competition to me is the ultimate. It's absolutely fantastic. I love racing against somebody else and proving myself stronger than him, making him suffer. It's really a challenge to me to make him go through hell as it were. I run them (marathons) fast because I find them more interesting that way. I find running hard boring enough. Running slow would just be out of this world."

At the Munich Games in 1972, Frank Shorter, running a 2:12:19, became the first American since Johnny Hayes in 1908 to win an Olympic gold medal in the marathon. Kenny Moore, fellow teammate and one-time American record holder in the marathon (2:13:27 in 1969), finished fourth. Later Moore wrote:

> When I was an Olympian, as my event—the marathon—approached, I prayed only to do my best, feeling that to hope for victory when there were 42 kilometers of rough road to cover was somehow presumptuous. I realize now that I was freed by this, that driving to the limit, with a full appreciation of the odds against winning, allowed me entry into a splendid region, filled

with wonderful performers, at peace even as we ran. When Frank Shorter won our race in Munich, he did not throw his hands skyward at first, but clasped them to his head, saying to himself, "My God, what have I done?" . . .

Frank and I sat in our room the next morning. It had been an effort of will to jog three miles around the soccer fields. . . . We were caught in the melancholy that follows a well-run race deepened now by the griefs of the Games. Neither of us said much, but the feeling persisted that something ought to be said . . .

"You know," I said, "all this time I thought the Olympic champion was somebody incredibly special."

Frank gave me a consoling look as though he would have liked to protect me from this final disillusionment. "And then you found out," he said, "that it was only me."

Clearly since then Shorter has become more than just somebody who runs marathons. As with Bikila, there is some special lightness and fluidity about the way he runs. This slender marathoner's build, set against the enormity of his achievement, has helped make him the king of marathoning in America. The boom in marathoning since Munich happened partly because of what he was and did.

Don Kardong, fourth-place finisher at Montreal, gets a chance to sit down after running the 1977 New York Marathon.

4

Montreal 1976

At the 1976 Montreal Olympics Frank Shorter ran the fastest marathon of his life, but lost to Waldemar Cierpinski, a twenty-six-year-old sports student from East Germany. The defending champion, one of the world's best-known marathoners, was beaten by a virtual unknown.

After the start in the stadium at Montreal, the pack of 67 took two laps around the track and then headed out along the loop course through the city streets. It was a warm, humid day with a constant, drizzling rain. After less than 5 kilometers, a leading pack of 15 had formed including Cierpinski, Rodgers, and Shorter. About 9 miles out, whipping along at slightly faster than five minutes per mile, the pack eroded to 10. Two Australians and a Swede dropped off within the next 3¼ miles. Shorter's first attempt to break away after 25 kilometers left only two runners able to follow—Cierpinski and Shivnath Singh of India, who later finished eleventh in 2:16:22. Lasse Viren of Finland, attempting a triple sweep after winning gold medals in the 5,000- and 10,000-meter races earlier in the week, gradually began to slide farther behind the lead pair (he eventually finished fifth in his first marathon race in 2:13:10).

Between 30 and 35 kilometers, Cierpinski began to pull ahead of Shorter, increasing his lead to 32 seconds with just over 2 kilometers to go. Over this last stretch of the course, he gained another 18 seconds, winning decisively in 2:09:55. Shorter was second in 2:10:45. Don Kardong, the third American on the Olympic squad, briefly held on to third place at the end until Lismont surged back, just managing to beat Kardong to the finish line in 2:11:12. Bill Rodgers, hampered by trouble with his right foot, had fallen back off the pace a bit more than halfway out. The last finisher was Lucio Guachalla of Bolivia in 2:45:31. Seven runners did not finish.

Kenny Moore was at Montreal, too, on assignment for *Sports Illustrated*. Moore and Shorter have run a number of marathons together. They finished the 1972 trials for the Olympic marathon in Eugene, Oregon, hand in hand, both faces lit by big smiles.

"If it had been ten degrees hotter, Frank would have won by two and a half minutes, because nobody can run in the heat like Frank. It still was the best race of his life, but we can't really know how hampered he was by the rain. The best he'd ever run was 2:10:30 in Fukuoka (Japan) and I was there that day. It was just three months after the Olympics and the Japanese were rooting him on and he went for it.

"I have never seen Frank anywhere looking as tired as he was at Montreal. We made a deal to talk so I could write my piece for the magazine. We had a little place to meet and he showed up, dank and sour. But he was so sweet in the formal press conference. Cierpinski got there first and was speaking in German through a translator, and Frank sat down wearily and blankly. Someone whose heart went out to him said: Would you like my earphones?

Frank said: No, I know what happened. And everybody laughed. Even then he was capable of self-deprecation. He must have been desperately tired. He really was not capable of giving me much. You're just absolutely at the end of your rope. You could have been on a raft for forty-eight days and starving to death and shown that kind of lassitude.

"By the next morning he'd recovered a lot. Somehow instinctively he knew, when he was that tired, I think, that he shouldn't say anything. He just smiled wanly and waited it out. Bad race, good race—if I finish a race I am so irritable, I am so mean that I have almost punched innocent people a couple of times with innocent requests because whatever it is can be so. . . . Nobody can put himself in your place at the end of a marathon."

The shock was Shorter's loss in a marathon, the first loss since his first marathon eight years before, after a remarkable series of victories. The pressure on the favorite in a race, where the odds are never a sure thing for anyone, was immense. Cierpinski seemed to emerge from virtually nowhere with no international reputation to precede him. Cierpinski was a product of the incredibly systematic and disciplined national effort the East Germans have launched in sports. In an article in a 1976 issue of *British Athletics Weekly*, he was quoted as saying:

> True enough, I was up front alone and ran by myself for some one-sixth of the race. But I do realize that my win was no solitary achievement. It was success borne out of the collective effort. The exacting preparations of the whole team, the work of our team doctors and masseurs, of my coach Walter Schmidt, of my fellow marathon runners—it all played an organic part. And so did the phenomenal performance of the GDR Olympic squad as a whole.
>
> "I was told to stick with the leaders," he said, "and this is precisely what I did. I was really happy to see that Frank Shorter's early bursts thinned out the leading group, but I found no real difficulty in staying with him."

The interviewer asked if he had felt the strain at any time during the race.

> Well, one tends to forget the hardships after a race and re-
> member only the good things. This is especially true after such
> a successful race. But nonetheless, it was hard, very hard. When?
> Well, I could not exactly say. Here and there. It always is.

One of the East German team's medical staff, Dr. Manfred
Hoppner, also had this to say about Cierpinski:

> I would praise his attitude to discipline above all. He never
> balked at doing exactly what he had been told in training, and
> strictly followed all dietary advice, subjected himself to all the
> prescribed massage and other treatment. He also kept himself fit
> psychologically, as instructed. . . . In his leisure time, he stayed
> in and quietly listened to records. He followed the daily routine
> as outlined to the dot."

Shorter has been the unofficial king of the sport since 1972. His
has always been the special name, the icon that invokes images of
a slender, intense young man with a mustache, thin and light, a
very fluid runner. Shorter himself, although inevitably affected by
the fame and adulation, is intensely uncomfortable about saying
too much about running. He hates to make it a big deal. Perhaps
it is enough that it already is so immensely important in his life,
the central passion to which he has devoted so much time and
energy. During the almost ten years since his undergraduate days
at Yale (he graduated in 1969 as a premed) he has developed his
great running talent in much more than just the marathon. "Most
distance runners don't have Frank's affinity for the short races or
his skill at them," Kenny Moore says. "Frank has got a wide range
of psychological sets. When he wants to run a good two-mile and
beat the hell out of Rod Dixon in the last half mile, he will have
an entirely different psychology from the one he has when he's
running a marathon."

In an interview Shorter generally talks easily and quickly about
what he has undoubtedly been asked many times before. People
who have met him or run with him remark on sometimes contra-
dictory characteristics: his friendliness, his aloofness, as well as his
informality and independence—a quality Moore once wrote about:

Frank Shorter, one of the greatest names in the history of running.

"There can be something hard in Shorter, a scornful quality, especially when he is out front and applying pressure." He is disarmingly funny, his humor edged with a kind of mock sarcasm. He can be keenly observant of small physical details about other runners. He has run 140 to 180 miles a week for years to be the

Frank Shorter's store in his home town of Boulder, Colorado.

best, but he also neither expects nor needs to win every race—although talking about Montreal eighteen months later made his voice sink. He shifted uncomfortably in his chair, rubbed his eyes, and after some answers let a defiant, challenging silence fill the air. There was a strong sense of sacred ground—questions he disliked as opposed to those he rolled with easily, something complex and unsettled beneath the informal demeanor. Away from questions and the tape recorder, out running along the streets of his adopted home town of Boulder under sunny wintry skies, the controlled tension vanished and his talk was genial, unassuming, and fun.

Along with his wife, Louise, and a nest of talented middle- and long-distance runners, Shorter operates a running store and a retail line of sporting goods that feature his name and his touch on the design as the selling point. The two-tone nylon running suits, the two-tone tank tops (one-half mesh for ventilation and one-half solid fabric), and the running shorts all carry a logo that features Shorter in illusory motion. The warehouse and nerve center of this enterprise are in a dumpy side of town near where the rail tracks cut through and where a few trailer homes mix in with newly built plant buildings. The office of Shorter Sports is extremely relaxed. The staff wear jeans, running shoes, and Frank Shorter warmup suits; one changing room holds a set of open wooden lockers stashed with everybody's running clothes. A shower and a toilet provide the final touches to this most unusual aspect of an otherwise familiar retail operation.

Shorter, the day of the interview, was sitting at one end of a long board-meeting-type table, his narrow face framed by a shaggy head of hair. Unlike the impression given by photographs, he is taller than imagined; his face is sensitive, full, wary, slightly puffy. On his right hand is a black and gold ring that he has worn for years. Smokey, a little brown and black dog, lay in one corner, sleeping.

"When I was about nine I wanted to be an Olympic ski racer. School was three miles on the outside of town and I liked to run anyway. I was also a cheapo—I could save the bus money. You

A drawing on a wall in Shorter's store.

see, I was on a very strict budget when I was a kid. I had nine brothers and sisters. I would get a certain amount to make it through the week and the bus cost so much and a hot lunch cost so much so I'd make my own lunch and run.

"Then I got sent away to prep school at Mount Hermon, which at that time had the best cross-country and distance running track teams of all the New England prep schools. They have a race there every year which is older than the Boston Marathon. It's the oldest continuous road race. It's called the Pie Race. Every year the whole faculty, the student body, everybody, would run this four-and-a-half-mile race. If you finished in under thirty-four minutes you got this huge pie, which you could put on your radiator or outside the window—it was in November—so it could last for a week. You know, when you're a kid in prep school and all the table heads are picking on you anyway so that you're not getting any desserts to speak of, that's an incentive. So I ran it. And the only guys to beat me were the first five guys on the cross-country team. To my way of thinking that was not bad since I had never trained at all."

Unlike many boarding schools where running has been for years the poor sister to football and baseball, Mount Hermon was a place that cared about its runners. On Saturdays the cross-country meets finished down the middle of the football field at half time. Although he was the New England prep school champion in cross-country and in the two-mile race in track, Shorter said, "I knew that didn't mean much in relation to the rest of the country."

Shorter chose Yale because of the good things he'd heard about Bob Giegengack, the running coach there, although he'd never seen the campus or Giegengack before arriving in New Haven the fall of his freshman year. Giegengack, who had been coach for the 1964 Olympic track and field team, was less than impressed with Shorter's initial dedication. He said Frank would run in the one-mile race, and would then ask if he was needed for the two-mile. If he wasn't, he would dash off skiing for the weekend. Shorter, a premed, was also an avid singer, but the shift in his priorities came toward the end of his stay at Yale when he asked Giegengack how good he could be. "I told him he could be the best if he wanted," Giegengack said later.

"I never ran during the summer until my senior year," Shorter said, "and that was really the year that I started to do well. That was the first time I'd ever really trained hard. I was up to about eighty miles a week at that point, running twice a day three or four times a week. The theory and workout schedules were always there; it was just a question of adding volume in terms of miles and then a few more intervals. Basically any kind of interval repetition/endurance training theory is the same. That's where luck comes in. I think the way Giegengack implemented it was the right way—for me.

"After Yale I got to go to Europe and room with Kenny Moore, who was also a big influence. I was an alternate at one meet and got to run a couple more and got my ass totally wiped, but I just got the feeling that the only difference between me and them was the amount of training I'd been doing. There wasn't some sort of mystical predisposition or genetic endowment or anything like that.

"I came back and ran out of money and dropped out of medical school. I came up here to Boulder and hung around because my wife was here in school at the time. I trained on the indoor track, pretty much just kind of bumming around that winter and then finished second in the AAU indoor. That's when I thought I could be relatively good.

"I never thought of a marathon until Kenny Moore talked me into running the Pan Am trials in Eugene in '71. I trained the same way as always, running around one hundred forty to one hundred sixty miles a week. It was a very windy day. I was all excited. I wanted to run hard from the start. Kenny kept talking me back. After about ten miles I couldn't stand it anymore and took off, and he came with me and we broke it open then. John Vitale came with us that day and we got rid of him after about thirteen miles. About three miles out from home we started into the wind. Kenny immediately tucked in behind me. I said: Aw, come on, you're gonna win. Don't do this crap. So we ran shoulder to shoulder and he eventually just pulled away and beat me by about a minute. I was dead.

"Steve Prefontaine was on the track. There was a twilight meet that day. He came up to me afterward and said: 'God, I'd never do anything like that. I don't know how you can do that.' 'Cause he was right on the track and he'd seen the faces on the people as they came in. And he said something like: 'God, that was stupid. You know, anybody who'd run that far is stupid.' I said: 'Well, I gotta make the team somehow!'

"I was more tired than I'd ever been from a long run, but I wasn't any more tired than I'd been on some of my hard track workouts. I got sick as hell afterward. I wanted to throw up. I haven't been sick like that since. I think your body's got to get sick once. I think there's actually some sort of adaptive process. Maybe it's mental. The first one's always just awful. Not so much during the race, but after."

Shorter, who says his habit of studying and noting the physical traits of his opponents is "just a personal thing," scoffs at the idea of "secrets." Everyone is fairly predictable in the way they run, he says, except for Lasse Viren, he notes wryly. "I'm not sure what Viren's weakness is. It's certainly not anywhere in the last mile of a race, which makes it pretty tough." It all comes down to running hard, he insists, and hoping that somebody else doesn't run better. On the day of a given marathon, if the start is slow, he may not know for a while just how he will do, but if the pace at the start is very fast, then he knows quickly what he is in for.

He enjoyed the Olympics in 1972 much more because "no one was particularly interested in what I was doing. It's not that you don't like the attention, because everybody's got an ego, but it's easier to get ready if you can just do it by yourself. I think that at a certain point it would be better just to declare a moratorium on all contact with the media. The only difficulty is pulling it off so that you don't come across as a misanthrope. Get it all out of the way and just concentrate."

Questions about the Montreal marathon in 1976 awaken a tangle of vivid memories. Shorter's voice turned soft when he recalled the "eerie" tension around an Olympic village. At first he says you create it yourself, and then he says you can just feel it anyway. "I don't think it's something you're making up. It's a good thing to have, if you deal with it right and use it to help you. You always get nervous so you might as well use it to help you run."

"When I was warming up, it was seventy degrees, the sun was shining, and it was humid. I was just sky-high. Maybe that made it a little harder, to come from the best of all possible conditions—for me—to pretty much the worst. It was raining while we were running around the stadium. It rained only on the first lane because the stadium ceiling covered the rest, and I found myself running in the second lane. I said, oh fuck, what are you doing this for, you're going to have to go the whole way in the rain. Gotta get wet sometime. I was just trying to put it off. I get very cold in the rain. It's more work.

"Other than getting stiff in the second half of the race, I actually felt very good. I was lucky because I had a very good day in terms of good days versus bad days. There was not that much distance between second and fourth, not much at all. But that showed how severe the conditions really were—the more adverse, the closer together everybody is. It takes much more effort to get away from someone because the diminishing return comes quicker in terms of the output you're using. One thing that hurt me is that I tried the kind of surging that I use when it's dry and I couldn't gain as much using the same effort. Probably my best chance would have been if the race had been about twenty-five miles. At about that point I pulled to within fifteen yards of Cierpinski and he got away again because I hit another bad patch."

Shorter has been asked repeatedly about running. He says his reaction to the questions depends on who's asking and why. Pedants, cocktail party buffoons, and people who aren't interested at all in the answer upset him. He appreciates the hunger to improve that impells many marathoners to ask a variety of questions, but anyone looking for common denominators for success is due to be disappointed. "I think there are certain starting points and from there you're on your own. If you can't deal with that, then it's just unfortunate for you." He has a special sympathy for questions from kids. "It's not so much information, but just the fact that they've gotten the guts to ask it, you know? I appreciate that because I would have been one of those kids when I was little that never would have been able to ask anything. So I'm sensitive to that. Everybody's got an ego and I kind of like it, in a way, but the ultimate end is to run and to run well. I don't think intellectualization has a hell of a lot to do with it. So I consciously avoid it. Maybe that's why I like running—I don't have to explain it. We're always being called on to explain things."

He emphasizes the individuality of the world's best marathoners and says it's useless to try finding labels for what explains their special physical and psychological characteristics. And he wonders if beyond being thin and having the right ratio of fast twitch/slow twitch muscles, anything meaningful can be said. "At this point if anybody knows, it's probably the East Germans and they aren't telling. But that's where we are. It's the state of the art—which is nowhere."

In a little less than three years Bill Rodgers has emerged as the newest icon in the running community. His Boston win in 1975 has given him the fastest American time ever and a tie for the fifth fastest in the world—2:09:55. His 1978 win at Boston was 2:10:13—just 18 seconds slower. He looks like a dreamer when he runs, wearing a pair of cotton gardening gloves to ward off the cold, his long fair hair blowing in the 12 mph wind, an all-consuming absorption in his gaze. He is the only other American marathoner to stand shoulder to shoulder with Shorter—or to race that way with him—with the two of them exchanging the order of one-two finishes in various road races and marathons on just about an even level. Rodgers's streak of speed over the past year has been astonishing, but he remains cheerful, seemingly unaffected, and extremely well liked by those who meet him.

His running career has had its fits and starts. He knew as a kid growing up in Newington, Connecticut, a town just outside of Hartford, that he had some ability as a runner. At Wesleyan College he ran track and cross country, where he termed himself a big fish in a little pond. His roommate during his sophomore year was lanky Amby Burfoot, winner of the 1968 Boston Marathon. His

Bill Rodgers, one of the world's top marathoners, discusses his running career in the back of his store.

reaction to the excitement of Amby's win and the calls that came in from around the world was one of interest, but it did not motivate him to try a marathon himself. On leaving college, Rodgers got involved in filing a conscientious objector application with his draft board. He moved to Boston to find a job at Peter Bent Brigham Hospital, from which he eventually got fired in 1971 for trying to bring in a union. Up till then he would run a little bit at the Huntington YMCA, lift weights, and smoke so much that he had to stop in the middle of some of his runs to catch his breath. Unemployment meant time for double workouts, and in 1973 he ran his first Boston Marathon, where he failed to finish. Improvement came in October 1974 where he ran a 2:28 at Framingham, Massachusetts. At Boston the next spring he made his mark. In 1976 he ran a disappointing fortieth in the Montreal Olympics, running a 2:25:14.

He is currently running about 145 miles a week, doing some Fartlek and a little bit of anaerobic training. Most of his training mileage is run at a 6:30 pace, though he may run as fast as 5:10 per mile going over hills. Prior to the 1975 Boston Marathon he was coached by Billy Squires, but he is now working with Bob Sevene, a coach for the Greater Boston Track Club. To get ready for a marathon, Rodgers likes to go up to 200 miles in one week, making it sound as if he just likes to touch that high point, extend himself a little farther to be absolutely sure how strong he is, and then back off to more moderate training levels.

Although he has a master's degree in special education and has worked at a state institution for the retarded, Rodgers now has his own running store in Brighton, just off Commonwealth Avenue where the Boston Marathon course snakes down a steep decline toward Cleveland Circle. The store bulletin board is filled with newspaper clips, announcements of races, clinics, all the chatter of the busy world of marathoning in the late seventies. Rodgers himself has a frantic schedule, with associate Russ McCarter trying to ride herd on all the people who want a piece of Bill's limited time. An interview with Rodgers takes place in the cavernous back room

Bill Rodgers of Melrose, Massachusetts, one of America's best marathoners, wins the 1977 New York City Marathon in 2:11:28.

amid cartons of Pepsi and running shoes. In person he seems to have the classic marathoner's blend of an almost frail frame (he is 5 feet 8 and 128 pounds) combined with something taut and hard. His features and fingers are delicate. His reputation is one of a cheerful, obliging soul who finds it very difficult to say no. But an altogether unheralded aspect to Rodgers is his intense competitiveness. He likes to win and he likes to beat the competition—he simply is easy in talking about it. He talks with zestful, slightly kooky drama, punctuating his talk with sudden shooshes, hmms, whistles, and sudden glints of humor.

"The 1976 Olympic trials—there was a lot of pressure. I was pretty confident of what I could do. I'm a very competitive person when I get on the roads and start running. I was pretty sure I could run pretty close to Frank. But making the team, how you're going to do in a race, jeez, who knows? For example, after about 8 miles Frank just suddenly made a break and Barry Brown went with him and I went with him, too, and I got a side ache right after that and I said, oh yeah, I screwed myself, why does this happen to me. The typical sort of thing, like a bad dream. And then once it went away I knew I was there and I felt very comfortable. We were running a 2:10 pace! But Frank didn't want to slow down at all. I got the impression from what he had said that he would cruise in real easy. He said, 'I'll walk in the last six miles if I've got it.' But he didn't want to slow down at all and my legs started cramping a little bit, so I slowed down the last mile or two. I knew where we were and the next closest people were a couple of minutes behind so I slowed down and Frank got in about seven seconds ahead of me. A lot of pressure there though. But I'm not the type of person who will get in a race and will suddenly go: I quit! and out like that. No one in the world scares me. No race scares me. The only thing that worries me somewhat is really intense heat. I think that that's nasty. I think running basically is to have fun. Sure it's hard work, but it's fun to some degree.

"At Montreal I'd been having trouble with the ball of my right foot—which I still have to this day. It's some kind of chronic injury. I don't know really what it is. Now it's in both feet. I ran in the ten-thousand-meter trial in June on a hard track in spikes, and after that my foot hurt. So I didn't do any speed work at all—one ten-thousand-meter race on July 4—and I did nothing all the way up to the Olympics. And you can't do that. I hadn't sorted things out as to what I needed to do to run a fairly good marathon. I also had the feeling that the Olympic marathon would not be that fast, that it would be an endurance race. I was running one hundred forty miles a week in the summer, which I thought was pretty good. I was stupid enough not to realize that you need anaerobic work no matter what the weather's going to be. I did try to run on the track once or twice and it hurt a lot, so I said, I don't want to screw my foot up. So I went to the Olympic camp where we were all staying and one of the few places to train was on a golf course. So every day I'd go there and run in the same shoes since I wasn't aware that perhaps it was the shoes that were the problem. Jack Foster had told me to run on grass because you get more spring when you get back on concrete. I think that aggravated my situation because of the little uneven bumps, you know? And then I would wear the same damn shoes when I walked around as leisure shoes. The trainers were using ultrasound on my foot. I was getting pretty bummed out, and I didn't want to talk to any people from the press. So I just left and stayed with my wife, Ellen, out in some Canadian's home. Then I cut my mileage down more than I normally would to see if the foot problem would go away. During the race I didn't feel the thing because I was so wound up at the time. All I was thinking was things like setting a new world record.

"There was a camaraderie among the marathoners before the start. But once the race started, once the gun went off . . . I remember I was next to Jack Foster and we were going up the hill out of the stadium and I said well, this isn't a bad pace, just hold this. We were going up this brutal hill after going around the stadium. Jack didn't say a damn thing. He was just dead serious. I'm gonna run and that was that. After that the only talk was when Shorter would come up to me and tell me to hold back a little bit, because I was moving ahead. I was pretty apprehensive. Once I got going in the race I didn't feel good at all. I didn't feel strong either. But I had enough strength so I could keep pushing for a while. Once I got tired, I got really tired. When the pack started to break up around twenty, twenty-five kilometers, Viren fell be hind me, but I was really hurting then. I knew he was going to come up and I knew I was going to get killed. I knew it was all over. He came up next to me; we ran together. I was really trying to gut it out, but I knew I was going nowhere. And I told him: you're a really tough runner, a very tough competitor. And he just kind of chortled or chuckled and moved ahead. What a tough runner!

"When I knew Viren was going to run after he had already gotten the gold in the five-thousand- and ten-thousand-meter events, and then he came into the room where all the marathoners were, I was furious. He thought he could get a medal when here were the best marathoners in the world and he's never even run a marathon and he thinks he's going to beat us. I said, there's no way I'm going to let this guy get out of the race without having to pay the price, learn what the marathon is about. And, unfortunately, he came through it pretty good!

"Frank and Don Kardong were both linked with the Nike Shoe Company at the time, working for Nike and wearing their shoes. They were both staying out at Nike and those two were more friendly in a way. I think Frank at that time considered me a rival, though I'm pretty sure he felt confident he could beat me. But I think that he was keeping his distance a little. On the other hand, he made a really nice gesture to me at opening day. He had an extra ticket for the opening ceremonies and those were hard to get. He sold me one for the normal price; he didn't up the price! But before the race Frank came into the room where we all were and we said good luck to each other and shook hands and everything. Kardong, too. We're basically friends, but there is a rivalry there as competitors.

"I was pretty bummed out after the race. I didn't run the next two days. And then after that I started training my ass off for New York. All I wanted was for Lasse Viren to be there—not just Viren but Shorter and everyone who'd beaten me in Montreal. There's so much emphasis on the Olympics as the ultimate measure of a runner. But I had a fantastic time there otherwise.

"The main thing that's helped me run well is a strong motivation. That's the primary thing, I think. If you really love it.

"Ideally, when I run I like to have someone three hundred yards ahead of me. I love chasing people. You know if I had a rabbit with little blinker lights the whole way that would be ideal. I

Don Kardong in his running store in Spokane.

always try to pull away before the end of the marathon. I'm a person who tries to crack the competition in the middle stages and almost never in my life have I been neck and neck with someone at the end of a marathon. If you are running against someone nearby you're constantly trying to push harder. I listen to his breathing. If he's behind me I listen to his footfall. If his footfall's suddenly getting faint, I'll become very determined and push as hard as I can for a while. In New York last year (1977) Garry Bjorklund and I were with some people in a pack about twelve to fourteen miles into the race. Then it turned into a two-man race. I sensed that he was very strong—he ran strongly all the way down First Avenue. I had been kind of weak until I started running down First Avenue. When I started down, I changed into a different runner. It was partly adrenaline. When I get carried away and feel good—watch out! It was like a duel. It happened very quickly when Garry fell back. I started to die near the end of the New York race. It had been fairly tough for me because there had been a lot of surging, a lot of back-and-forth crazy stuff. After I left Bjorklund, I checked out where he was. I constantly look over my shoulder. I'm not worried—if people see me look over my shoulder and think that I'm weak, then I got news for 'em! I never worry about that stuff. I always worry about people passing me. If they've passed me then I don't enjoy it. In New York I gained very rapidly on Garry. Then it was just a question of whether I would fall apart or not. There was five miles to go and I concentrated on running efficiently, no hard pushing, keeping my eye on who's behind me. In a marathon everyone's dying the last six miles. Everyone's getting obliterated. And you are, too, though if you've got the lead during the last few miles of a marathon it can be a big advantage. You've got the press truck there—that helps psychologically. Meanwhile, I'm getting closer and closer to the finish and thinking, oh, I'm almost there. Victory can be very sweet in a marathon. It can be very sour when you get nailed, I tell you. That's a funny thing.

"I can remember I ran the Kyoto marathon and there were huge crowds there. Of course, they were all yelling in Japanese, but I'd hear my name. They're really gung-ho about the marathon there. Near the end I came to a water stop and took a drink. I think this stopping really freaks the Japanese out. You make it or you die—there's no surrender. They started shooting off firecrackers outside the stadium, but I was so obliterated the crowd just didn't exist for me. I may as well have been running down the back yard. I just didn't care about it. When you're wiped out, all you care about is water and survival—it's down to pretty basic things."

Eighty years after a now-forgotten Hungarian runner named Kellner took fourth in the first Olympic marathon, Don Kardong also ran fourth in an Olympic marathon. For Kardong, the margin between fourth and the third-place bronze medal was just over three seconds. His entry in the books now looks as dry as Kellner's. Finishers outside the hallowed top three are not widely encouraged to share their experiences. But no single marathoner's account of a race is any more complete than another's. Not even the winner, who depends on the shadows behind him to give him substance, can do more than offer valuable clues to the mystery of each race that flashes by so rapidly every time.

Kardong was the kid on the team, the dark horse at the Olympic trials in Eugene, Oregon, two months before. Apart from a brief boyhood stint running to his grandmother's house in Bellevue, Washington, 4 miles from his own home, he never bothered with running until his sophomore year in high school. His basketball coach suggested he run on the cross-country team to stay in shape through the fall, which Don thought was "a dumb idea." Quick success was followed by little improvement in his junior and senior years, which "was very much of a disappointment to me. I thought running was boring. And I didn't enjoy the pressure on me to continue to do as well as I had before."

Although he ran cross country and track for four years at Stanford, where he was a psychology major, Kardong never thought he would pursue running beyond college. He had shown a measure of his potential in his junior year during the nationals in Des Moines, where he finished fourth behind Burkele, Prefontaine, and Bjorklund in the 3-mile race. In his senior year he almost beat Prefontaine in a 3-mile race, running his best time to date: 13:20, just over a 4:26 minute per mile pace. Then his plans began to change.

"I had this feeling of being on the brink of world class. I read what Shorter said and I didn't want to ask myself that maybe I could have been. The only way to find out is to put some time into it. I went back down to the Stanford area in 1971 and lived very cheaply. I just trained, consistently running more than one hundred miles a week."

Although his racing times improved, a bout of mononucleosis

10 FREE REPORTS!

The **10 FREE <u>RUNNER'S WORLD</u> Running Reports** make running easier and more fun than ever! Discover shoe secrets, special tips for women, how to train for your next race, how to make time to run and stay motivated, super nutrition, injury prevention, and so much more!

10 FREE GIFTS!

 30% Post Consumer Waste
Printed on Recycled Paper.

before the 1972 Olympic trials zapped his strength. Kardong found himself being lapped in the 10,000-meter trials. With only one marathon (a 2:18) behind him, he elected to run the trials for that one, too. Watching Galloway and Bacheler hang back until the midpoint of the race made a deep impression.

"I just had this feeling they knew what they were doing, and it had quite a bit of meaning for me four years later. Everyone is so excited to be in the Olympic trials they go out really fast. I used the exact same strategy in '76. Was it hard to miss the Olympics then? It was and it wasn't. I was prepared for it. I didn't take it as a personal insult from God.

"The overseas international competition that followed was good experience. When you run with the best in the U.S., it's still just the U.S. When it's with the best in the world, you realize you're at the top of the pack. Once you've done that you have a different way of perceiving yourself. It's a great feeling.

"I think that for a lot of people—and I know it was true for me—making the team was the goal, and you feel good about having done just that. You could contrast that with someone like Shorter. For him making the team was an expectation. He had to do that to go on to win a gold medal. So I think there are two types of attitudes you can take in to the Olympics. One is to go along for the ride; and the other is to go along for a medal. Originally my intention was to go along for the ride, and yet as I started to rethink the whole thing I thought, well, I get a ride no matter what and now I may as well go for a medal, too.

"Evaluating yourself is hard. But I said I guess I don't look like a very likely bet for a medal because I just barely made the U.S. team. But I had this feeling I'd gone out too slow at Eugene. If I went out a little bit faster I could pick up maybe a minute, a minute and a half, which would put me within striking distance of the best in the world. If I unfolded the right strategy I thought I could be up there with those people.

"You know, it's a very strange thing. I was conceding the race to Shorter, I think, and I should have conceded it to Rodgers really, but I didn't because I wasn't as awed by him for some reason. Basically because I hadn't run against him as much. Anyway, I conceded that Frank was going to win and what I was intending to do was move up through the back and sneak up once again for a third or—well, third was what I really had in mind. I talked to Kenny Moore and to my coach and we decided the same thing. What I had to do was adjust my first ten miles and run a little bit faster, but with the same basic idea of not going out too fast, and then later picking up enough to run well. I was about ready now to run a little slower than a five-minute-per-mile pace.

"Those last two months I ran one hundred ten to one hundred twenty miles a week, running pretty much on my own. I did a lot of thinking about Montreal on the run, deciding strategy and everything else. In going to the Olympics I told myself that I may do poorly, but at least I'm going to have a good time while I'm there. I was fighting the whole time to keep from letting it become too serious because it just destroys it for me, when you've got to worry about it, thinking that the fate of the country rests on this race. Honestly, a lot of people consciously or unconsciously feel that way. I tried to be realistic about realizing that it was only a race and whether I did well or bombed out was not going to really matter, and whenever I can really achieve that feeling I run well. At the same time it's almost impossible to do that because of all the frenzy and intense feelings focused on the Olympics.

"Generally when you're in distance running you get ignored. Any amateur athlete is ignored most of the time. Suddenly when you're on the Olympic team everybody wants to touch the hem of your robe. It's bizarre, it really is. I found it kind of humorous and yet I honestly enjoyed it. I mean it's not that I just enjoyed the praise, but I enjoyed being asked to a banquet and to say a few words. You can say whatever you want and people really don't care too much. My own reaction was well, sure, if you want to make me your hero for the day, that's fine with me, just so long as we both realize that this is all kind of an artificial game. When you make something a game, it can be a lot of fun. I had a lot of fun at the Olympics. Boy, some of those guys would hole them-selves up in their room and worry about their race for two solid weeks and go off and just blow it. Of course I could say that because I didn't have any pressure on me. I was not a favorite. If I'd finished the race on my feet people would have said congratu-lations. I'll never be able to do that again.

"Both Frank and Bill, I think, tried to stay isolated. Bill, partic-ularly, wasn't visible at all. Frank got kind of nervous, worse and worse as the time approached. I think both of them recognize the kinds of things I'm saying here, that it was not going to be good for their race to be that worried, but when they're in their posi-tions, it's hard to control.

"I'm usually able to sleep before a race, but I began to get very nervous the day before. The night before, we drove around the course, that is, myself, my mother and sister, my coach and his family, my girl friend and some of her family. It took us about an hour and a half to drive around the course. I couldn't believe I was going to run around it. But I began to get pretty nervous and to withdraw into myself. People sensed that and were very nice to me.

"The day of the race was almost just like a blur, especially leav-ing the Olympic Village to go down to the track. I was numb with the excitement of it. I really enjoyed it because I felt like I was at the center of the world. I knew that there were more important things going on, but everyone was watching the Olympics and at this point the Olympics was the marathon, so everyone was zeroed in on this and you got this sense of how many people must be watching. It was exciting. It really was exciting. It was just kind of a suspended animation all that time until the race started.

"I believe the way to run the marathon is to stay mentally relaxed the first ten miles and to hold a little back from your fastest pace. I force myself to run easy. I tell myself: drop back, quit fighting the pace, be efficient. But I was also trying during those first ten miles to get my mind off the race, because I think you can kind of float through with no mental effort at all and save the mental effort for when you need it. So what I was doing was looking for my friends in the crowd. My mother has this picture of me waving to her right before the mile mark.

"I think I was with the leaders for about three miles, and then I forced myself to drop back and gradually let them go.

"The crowd was incredible the whole way. It thinned out a little after about fifteen miles and then picked up for the last five. There were times when people were four deep on both sides of the road. The funny thing is that when you come by they yell for you, which is the only time they're actually yelling. But your sensation as you run is of people yelling for over two hours. You have this constant roar in your ears. I did use it as energy. There was a danger in using that energy and going too fast too early, which I had to fight. It can also be a hindrance, too, like the New York marathon coming down First Avenue and people were on both sides leaning in so that you almost felt like you were going to get crushed. Of course people move out of your way as you get closer, but you have this sense that you're forcing them back like a plow. It's really mentally draining. There were a couple of places like that in Montreal and it was a little scary.

"I let about thirty guys go at the start so I didn't know what place I was in. And I was hoping that someone would yell you're in twelfth place or whatever, but no one did. At about fifteen miles this kid comes up on a bike and says: 'Who's winning?' I was almost angry. It was really strange to be running and passing other runners and not knowing how many more I had to catch before I was up there with the leaders. I knew I was getting pretty close. Somewhere about eighteen miles into the race someone said: 'You're thirty seconds out of third place.' I looked up and I saw a group of runners. I didn't know if that was who they meant or if there were guys beyond that. As I started to catch them somebody said: 'You're six seconds out of a bronze medal.' Then I knew that was the group I had to catch. That was Viren and Lismont and Drayton. I knew Viren, but I didn't recognize the other two. I worked to try to catch them for two or three miles. Finally, at one of the aid stations, they slowed down just a little bit to get something to drink. I caught all three of them right there. I knew I had to keep moving away from them then or else. I knew I had to look strong and keep moving, because I knew to have somebody catch you at that stage of the race is demoralizing and if I could demoralize them they wouldn't stay with me.

"And then since my whole objective had been to move into third place and I had finally gotten it, there was almost a mental and physical letdown. One of my legs cramped suddenly, and mentally I had a lot of trouble maintaining my pace. I was reading my name in headlines in the Spokane papers, and then at about twenty-five miles I heard footsteps. It was Lismont who had made this comeback. When he caught me I was trying to stay with him until we started downhill and he just quickly moved away, and I just could not stay with him. My legs just couldn't take the downhill. I was hoping that I would get back down to the track once we were on the flat and I would catch him again. I guess I cut the distance by about half, but he was just too far ahead. He beat me by three-point something seconds.

"After the race I was really excited to have finished fourth, but having been so close to getting a medal I was really disappointed at the same time. Why couldn't I have held on a little longer, you know. I'm really not clear in my own mind what my feelings were. I felt very relieved at just being able to stop. But whether I was pleased or displeased—it was a little bit of both. What I did tell myself—in fact, I was aware of this from the moment I heard his footsteps behind me—was that I had better give it everything I had or I was going to regret it the rest of my life. When I got done with my race I made a quick evaluation of how hard I had tried that last part. I think I was very realistic in saying that I had given it everything I had and that was good because I didn't get three days down the road and say, well, maybe I could have run a little faster, because I really couldn't have.

"It was also the most complete exhaustion I've ever felt. Of course, it's a totally different feeling from what you experience on a hard three-mile run. You've got about three different kinds of exhaustion. Your fluid levels are low so you're cramping; you've pounded so hard that you get sore muscles; and you've had to concentrate on the race so hard that you're exhausted mentally as well, so everything is just—psshuuu! It's a total sense of exhaustion and it's really taken me a long time since the Olympics to build things up from that low.

"The first person I spoke to was Frank. Of course I didn't even know who had won. Frank said: 'Helluva race.' 'Did you win?' I asked. 'No, I got second.' I could tell he was really bothered by it. When I had passed Billy, we grunted. I felt very strange passing him—I was surprised he was there. I thought something was wrong. He's not the kind to make excuses or to give up.

"It's funny now in this town to have the little kids put you on this pedestal. People don't always treat you the way they should— they are too nice to you.

"I've seen a lot of people that I've run against in high school or college who've quit who I really think had more talent than I have. Sometimes they just get tired of it like I was in high school. Sometimes they get married and have responsibilities that inhibit them. Sometimes they get injured. That's very common. So I think people who survive with a degree of talent and then put that together with the right training are able to succeed, but I don't think it's just the training factors. I've seen a lot of people work awfully hard without the same degree of success.

"Sometimes I wonder which comes first, whether you get the success and then develop the psychological makeup that follows, or vice versa. Obviously people like Frank and Bill have quite a bit of confidence in their own ability—that may just be a matter over the years of having success in those things. But I think that anybody who's running competitively at distances has a certain intensity about being able to put themselves through a training regimen. There's simply a certain amount of discipline involved. Bill Rodgers is a very easygoing guy but very intense in the way he trains and what he'll put himself through. And that's essential.

"I enjoy the whole aspect now of being able to travel and seeing friends and competing with the best and that kind of thing. It's not particularly exciting to think about having that gradually taper off. I think you can approach running one of two ways. You can approach it competitively and try to be one of the best, or you can turn around and do it for fun and relaxation. I think that when I sense I'm not able to do the first, I'll switch to the second.

"Having this store is a very convenient way to make a living and train at the same time. I don't tend to look too far in the future with it, whether it'll be a constant or if I'll move into something else. I like writing. I tend to think the same thing as I did about the running. Maybe I can be a good writer, maybe I'd be the shits. There's only one way to find out and that's by trying to do it."

5

On the Road

There are some simple questions both runners and crowds ask silently, implicitly, by their very presence. Will they do it? How fast will it be? How will they finish—freshly or in pain? And runners wonder exactly the same thing. For runners the elation at being in the public eye is mixed with the apprehension of not doing well. But there is another aspect as well, a fundamental respect that draws the crowd to watch and is saved for the tagalongs and the stragglers at the end. They tried, they did it, and often as not someone watching cares. It is not apparent quite so much in the shorter road races, the tune-ups, the four-milers, the six-milers, the ten-milers, as it is in marathons or ultramarathons. The world comes to watch an expression of energy in a particularly vivid format. We have said we will cover this terribly long distance, and then by concentrating, by firing our wills, making ourselves run, we exclude and deny all the other choices that make us fantasize in races about lying down, going home, walking off the course, wondering as everyone does at some point—why am I here? Hardly anyone stops. The unwritten code dictates finishing, no matter how slowly or how far back. Walk if you have to, but finish. The crowd senses the struggle, the negative forces that lurk underfoot, the snares that the flashing feet of runners evade with every stride. The longer the race, the more faces grow weary. The patter of applause from the small knot of people at a short road race is a little louder for the top finishers, the cream of the pack. There are still good words for the rest, but it is not too intensely expressed. But when the distance is a marathon everyone is accorded equal respect. Every finisher becomes heroic for a brief moment as he hurries, as fast as he can, into the cleared electric space where all lines converge, where timers and friends wait, where some mythical beast, some made-up entity called "finishing," dwells. But what does the crowd care if you ran 42:28 or 43:28? They simply don't notice such insubstantial units of time. Alas for the runner who runs a slower time than normal. A girl friend rushes forward to congratulate some man, who—hands on hips, eyes dark, mouth open for more air—shakes his head. "I just blew up out there," he says, filled with contempt for himself. Runners can be maniacal. They are greedy to do well, and in this man the simple animal satisfaction of stopping, the simple spiritual reward of having gone the distance, has not yet surfaced or is lost. Our friend rejects, for the moment, the pleasure others take in what he has done. He knows he could have run faster. Such scrupulousness commands some respect, and yet it is also a little comic. "I got a p.r.!" they say proudly, a personal record. To the crowd it makes no difference. The runner alone treasures such seconds. Two separate sets of perceptions are involved between runner and spectator. There is always the space between those who have done it and those who have not. An embrace is for the bastard you managed to beat out in a terrible dash to the finish. Who else can understand, even imperfectly, just what that day really meant? It depends on the intimacy of men and women who normally might never talk to one another—truck drivers, bankers, shipping clerks, poets, accountants, cooks, attorneys, teachers, the unemployed, children. It is a democracy of shorts and T-shirts. This is not to say that snobberies of talent and competitiveness do not flourish as well in such human soil. In the late sixties and early seventies, runners invariably gave a wave when passing in opposite directions, as truckers in Latin America might. They were the new cowboys of the empty spaces, surrounded by bellowing cars and bleating pedestrians. Now in congested urban areas too many runners have blurred the special distinction. They threaten by their very numbers to become another kind of pollution.

A race in New York City's Central Park on a December morning is about to begin. The day finally decides to let the winter light blaze through the growing rents in the clouds. Dozens of brightly clad men and women gyrate like marionettes as they dance near the starting line to keep warm. Every face is sharp and distinct; the air chatters with images—a man jumping on his toes to keep warm; the egomaniac no one has noticed before running bare-chested and bare-legged in the 20-degree weather; a runner's boyfriend taking the ski parka she hands him; dozens of faces making a crowd. There is the usual gossip: "Did you see Michael's time in the five-miler last week? Fantastic is what it was . . . how do you like those shoes? . . . I told her a divorce settlement is not . . . it's two laps around minus the Harlem Hill." Kurt Steiner, of the Road Runners Club, irrepressibly loquacious, speaks into a loudspeaker that turns his voice into crackle. Few understand; most press in like anxious cattle toward the starting line. At the front, the top competitors inhale frosty air, remote to one another even when they smile or wish one another luck; the square paper numbers pinned to their chests catch the light. An undercurrent of tension catches everyone up. The officials glance at their watches, at one another. Friends, lovers, grandmothers, curious dog walkers, hurry themselves and fan out on each side of the roadway, cameras ready. The empty lanes stretch out, open and flat. The runners in the back of the pack can see nothing but the backs of legs, legs garbed in wonderfully maniacal panoply—knee socks, ribbed thermal underwear, lavender tights, and occasionally just very pink skin. For a viewer far down the roadway those last few seconds pass slowly. Human cooperation is made manifest; a community of interest keeps everyone silent, gathered together to do something in common, each runner earnestly opposing the others. For the marathoner the race is homework, another test. The gun fires and the centipede's legs blaze into motion. The multiheaded thing jiggles forward growing a lance of the bravest and fastest who hug the curb and drive out in front. As this mobile community approaches, it resolves itself into individuals. They pass in an almost hypnotic silence. Yet inside each runner's mind buzzes a swarm of feelings and sensations, which, for him, is the only reality, the only thing he can hear.

At ultramarathons the crowds, though normally quite small, applaud and cheer with a special fervor every finisher who comes in. To run 50 miles and to finish, no matter how slowly, is to survive something special. It is as if the runners have dived under water and are out of sight except for an occasional heel breaking the surface. One waits five, six, seven hours, lap after lap, as they push on. Spectators feel particularly helpless and uneasy. What do you say to someone who's in his forty-third mile and looking terrible? So they say just: "hey, looking good," or "way to go," but if their friend is struggling they might say nothing. One ultrarunner said his friends never tell him when he looks terrible, but he can see it in their faces. "It angers me," he said, "because at that point if I *am* suffering I just want support. I don't need to know the truth."

When at last an ultramarathon is over, acclaim greets every runner. The ordinary feeling of separateness among strangers is suspended for a few seconds. The spectators applaud the endeavor, share the satisfaction every runner has that at last this, too, has ended. Someone you might know, maybe by name, maybe not, when you shuffle along, hobble-legged, walking with a sailor's rocking shoreside gait, will catch your eye and smile and say: "That was wonderful."

Chris Stewart, suffering from bleeding feet, holds on for a third place finish at 1976 New York City Marathon.

There is a popular misapprehension about marathons that equates the race with immense pain and suffering. It can be very hard on a friend or relative to see someone they know under normal circumstances as a cheerful soul storm over the line, face set, the sides of the mouth caked with dried saliva. One runner weeps, another lies down among the leaves, a woman peels off bloodied socks. And marathoners are often the biggest crybabies and hypochondriacs imaginable. In the days preceding a race there is often a fair amount of commentary about stool consistency, pains in the ankle, and the inability to sleep well. On the drive to the race, tension over being on time or taking a wrong turn can lead to temper flashes. Runners themselves love to complain to one another out of their habitual narcissism. "Well, I don't feel so well. Jeez, I don't know what it is, but my hamstrings have been knotting up. I'd like to run at a 5:45 pace, but I just don't see how I can do it." One's own injuries seem catastrophic—even one's mates can't quite share the same pitch of concern. Complaining provides a cover, too, allowing one to establish a reasonable excuse after bagging a poor performance. And it is bound in with some superstitious feeling that excessive confidence will be punished. Runners are childlike and brave, impossibly serious and recklessly indifferent to the rigors and pains they sometimes encounter.

Change is one of the inescapable themes of running. It isn't that change doesn't surround everyone, including marathoners in their hours away from running, but the running itself, the preparations for it, its effects, the rewards—all these are clearly and precisely in flux. After all, movement, which is made visible only by change, is as basic to running as breathing. The motion comes from some imprecisely charted inner space. It is nothing to run one step, five steps, or fifteen, but beyond half a minute, something else begins, something that separates the runner from the nonrunning world. Steady motion commences; the familiar landmarks of a run appear and disappear. Underfoot rolls the road; passing cars slide by. Breath breathes. Thoughts flicker over the face of the world, sometimes carry one so totally that the running is no longer noticed.

Runners trail out along the course of a 1977 marathon at a navy depot in Me-chanicsburg, Pennsylvania.

The mileage counter in the brain ticks on; mental images of old runs intrude on the present one. As enough time goes by, the runs of a year or five years ago begin to recede from memory. You never get back to them. Friends drop out of running. New ones join. Old ones stay and get older. Johnny Kelley, four-time winner of the Boston Marathon, although now in his seventies, can still run respectably well in the middle of the pack. It doesn't matter what you did; it's what you do now. The running, like one's life, just keeps changing till the end.

There are as many answers to why people run marathons as there are marathoners. Everyone's story is different, and what each has to say is only part of the truth. It never seems possible to send a plumb line all the way down to the bottom. The riverbed is too murky, too mutable, and ultimately too remote to perceive more than dimly.

"I'm not worried about numerical age," insists Harry Cordellos, forty years old, an information clerk for the Bay Area Rapid Transit System in San Francisco. Harry, who thrives on challenges, calls marathon running "a tremendous confidence builder." Harry happens to be blind, and has been so since 1954. He has simply found ways to do what he wants to do. It has required ingenuity, but he has had enough of that to run almost forty marathons.

"I've been running since the midsixties, but in 1968 I started running seriously. My brother ran the Dipsea race out here. I decided that if he could do it with a more than two-hundred-pound frame, then I could, too. I began to find partners to run with. I often have to change partners, but I have a pool to choose from. The trouble is I can't always make a training schedule to run the way I want. It's frustrating if someone misses or can't make it with me, and I sometimes have many weeks of skimpy mileage. For a marathon I try to push up to sixty-five to seventy miles a week.

"When I first started, my partner would carry keys and I'd chase their sound around a track. He'd be in the first lane and I'd be in

Fritz Mueller, forty-one, holds the Master's record (for runners over forty) in the marathon with a 2:20+ at Boston in 1978.

the second lane. One day I took a bad fall. So we tried bumping elbows—one more refinement—and ran in stride. I'd feel body movement right through his arms, so we'd get a steady rhythm going. I only grab wrists when we make a turn. My partner will call out the curbs—all that stuff. Now I can run *out* of rhythm with someone else.

"I was born with glaucoma, and by the time I was in high school I'd had fourteen eye operations. You know, for me, contrary to what people think, being blind is not being in darkness with no ray of sun. It's sickening to hear that stuff. I just tell them I couldn't run one step in the dark. I can't say that I see darkness. I could never visualize a wall of blackness. I have my own images of the world from when I could see. I visualize things normally and my mental image of the world is complete and surrounds me totally.

"The 1970 Golden Gate Marathon was the first one I ran in. My time was three hours and fifty minutes. I've run only one sub-three-hour race. That was a 2:57:42 at Boston in 1975. I was able to run the race like everyone else for all practical purposes. My goals in running are two. One is to run in the Olympic marathon in a section for the blind or handicapped. The second is—I'm Greek—to run the Greek marathon that goes from Marathon to Athens.

"I have other interests, too, like camping, swimming, and waterskiing. I expect to set up an arrangement to ski through a slalom course by getting directions from the boat via a fourteen-watt megaphone. The only thing that troubles me is that I get a little down about injuries—that's all. The runners I've met—you couldn't ask for better people. In ordinary social circles, I just don't find people as sincere."

Walt Stack, a seventy-year-old hod carrier, lives on Collingwood, one of the steepest streets in San Francisco. A warmhearted man who casually laces blasphemies into his speech, Walt thrives on physical challenges. He gets up weekdays at 2:30 A.M., bicycles down to the bay and goes for a long swim in water that may get as cold as 46 degrees. Next he sets off on a shirtless 17-mile run, which brings him back to the bathhouse. He then jumps onto his trusty three-speed to get to work. A hod carrier lifts 80 to 100 pounds of cement in his hod innumerable times a day. Walt's life has been a hard one. He hopped freight cars when he was thirteen or fourteen; worked on a goat ranch and in a Texas circus; joined the Army at fifteen, went AWOL, rejoined later, and was thrown into a stateside brig for his earlier absence; shipped out on coal-burning ships; and worked on the kill floor of San Francisco slaughterhouses. Walt is president of the Dolphin South End Runners Club, whose motto "Start Off Slow and Taper Off" indicates the kind of free-wheeling democracy of talent that belongs to the club. Walt has been particularly interested in encouraging women to run and in making the less talented feel there is room for them as well. Walt has run many marathons and ultramarathons, slowly but steadily. He has a definite kind of offhanded eccentricity to his way of doing things. His chest and arms bristle with tattoos, and one wall of a room in his house where he keeps trophies and pictures of himself in races is chock-full of buttons representing every left-wing cause imaginable.

"Of course the most common question raised is why do you do it? And, of course, I try to be honest with myself. On an amateur level the average man who's been involved for any length of time, a decade or more, in long-distance running is involved primarily because of his ego. Now when I say that I don't mean to use the word in its negative sense but in the sense of his personal self-esteem. Most people will be reluctant to admit that this is a primary motivating factor, but when you come right down to it, that's really what it amounts to. Of course, he gets pleasure from running, health benefits, therapeutic aspects, all these things are important, too. The bad thing is that you can't acknowledge that you get some little kick out of the praise you get in life; it just doesn't sound right. I guess society has developed a certain attitude toward it— it's considered immodest. Now I never have been a man who makes a principle of humility. Not that I'm a blatant egotist either. I don't

Walt Stack, a seventy-year-old San Francisco hod carrier, explains why every morning he swims in the bay and runs 17 miles before going off to work.

believe in making a big horse's ass of myself. Now, I figure I'm an old man, but even with one foot in the UC med school pickling vat and one on a banana peel, I'll outrun all these kids. Now I don't mean that they couldn't run rings around me if they practiced one-tenth the time I did, but the point is, they don't, see. And so all these people are saying to me, 'Hey, Jesus, that's good.' That's a great feeling, you know."

On a cold January evening, Jim Pearson, possessor of the fastest official 50-mile time ever run by an American, goes out to the barn to feed the horses at his home in Bellingham, Washington. Like a lot of runners, Pearson is as comfortable in warmups and running shoes as others are in jeans and shirts. One of the horses turns a dark eye on two strangers, but Jim, unconcerned, fills the feedbox and then leads the way back to the main house. A high school teacher, married to one of his former students, Janet, Jim has a boyish, lighthearted manner. The study next to the living room seems entirely given over to running. In addition to the pictures, plaques, and bowls are back issues of *Runner's World* in bound volumes. On October 25, 1975, at the age of thirty-one, in Seattle, Pearson ran 50 miles in 5 hours 12 minutes 41 seconds, a pace of about 6:14 minutes per mile. There is a small color photograph of the finish in his scrapbook. It isn't the runner's face but that of a relative, an older woman with snowy hair, that stands out. She is yelling something, delighted, as intensely *there* as the runner himself. It is charming and moving. Why him? Jim says he isn't sure. There are better runners around. Maybe he has a strong constitution. His aunt says he is a typical bullheaded Taurus. "All my neighbors thought I'd never make it because all they ever heard me do was cough.

"In school I somehow had to find my place, and athletics was it. My father isn't a high school graduate, and he really didn't push me to do well academically. My grade average was just okay in high school and in college, so athletics was the only place to impress some of my relatives, the male types, who I needed to impress as a kid. I did that, I did pretty well in the long jump and I loved basketball, but I wasn't too good. . . . I hated football, but it might have been my best sport. I'm out there every day. I mean even when I quit racing I go out and I run at least fifty miles a week— except for that one time when Janet was sick. I think it's fun.

"I set goals. I guess I'm really goal-oriented. I have mileage goals. I would like to run a two-hundred-mile week this year, just to see if I could do it."

Brian Maxwell, a Canadian, is a world-class runner. His current best was a 2:15:14 at the biennial Enschede marathon in The Netherlands in 1977, a course record set in 78-degree heat. He is a strong candidate for the Canadian Olympic team for the 1980 Games, and he seems poised on the edge of being not just among the top but among the very best. His apartment is on the top floor of a small apartment building in Berkeley, California. He is getting a graduate degree in exercise physiology and working as an assistant track coach for the University of California track team. He was graduated from U of C in 1975 with a major in architecture, which, as he put it, "was not very compatible with being a world-class marathoner. It's very demanding in terms of time as well as mentally. Doing forty hours a week in the studio and trying to run one hundred miles a week! Well, my running suffered from it."

His apartment faces south, looking out on the hills on the other side of the bay, the city of San Francisco, and the Golden Gate Bridge. His apartment is simple bachelor funk. As he talks, he makes a poached egg, which ends up on top of a couple of slices of bread. He cuts the bread into cubes and dibbles it around in the egg yolk, talking steadily. He has sandy hair, is extremely intense, both reserved and friendly. Waiting and deciding quietly. He's confident, thoughtful; having tasted some success, he is near now, very near to doing better things, but he remains controlled. Later he heads up to a nearby track to watch a development meet on the sparsely filled benches, half-watching the meet under the bright California sunshine and then, when he is really engrossed by one of the questions, turning away to look at the interviewer.

"There's some top marathoner—maybe Zatopek—who said that the most important thing in a marathoner is a strong will. I've always been very stubborn. Being a youngster growing up in Canada, in Toronto, the big thing was ice hockey, and I always wanted to be a hockey player. I'd go out and play five, six, seven hours a day during the winter. Even then the way that I'd play was that I'd never give up. I'd play for hours and hours, and everyone else would want to stop. It was always that way. The first time I ran I was in the ninth grade. I just knew that's what I wanted to do. The next fall in high school I really started to train for the first time. What appealed to me about it was that I could train whenever and wherever and as often and as hard as I wanted. I didn't need anybody else. It fitted the old Protestant work ethic of the more work you do the more rewards you get.

"In college I thought a lot about my training. I increased the quality while keeping the distance about the same. I was running only about ninety to one hundred miles a week. I began to stop worrying about mileage and to stop plodding. I got into the hard-easy system that I use now.

"I've progressed with that system. I've moved to more of an extreme than even Bowerman's system suggests. I try to go absolutely as hard as I can on a given day in terms of distance and speed. For instance, yesterday was a fairly typical day. I ran twenty-one miles in the morning. I stopped a couple of times, but it took me two hours and eight minutes. It was a six-minute pace basically. In the afternoon I did about six miles in thirty-five minutes and then went straight on to the track where I did twenty-five 220s with a 110 jog. I try to run those really hard, doing the 220s in thirty to thirty-two seconds. The 110 goes very fast when you're slowing down and then accelerating. And then I jogged a couple of miles after that. So I got in about thirty-three miles. Today is an easy day. I run once, six to ten miles, depending on how I feel. Sometimes I do repeat hills instead of the track. Sometimes I just do another distance run. I get three hard days a week.

"One of the reasons this training works for me is that besides being stubborn I'm also very impatient. I get bored as hell running slow. I also hurt a lot more when I run slow because the energy's going up and down. If I'm running hard, then I'm sort of free, I'm going for it. I prefer to run on my own. Sometimes I run with my girl friend on slow runs and that's nice. When I'm by myself I race by myself and I really push myself. If I have someone to talk to, then I don't mind running slow. I'd go crazy trying to run any slower than a 6:30 pace by myself.

"There's no real fascination to me about a 2:12. I know I can do a 2:12. There's a fascination to 2:08! My future times will improve with a few more years of maturity and more of the training I'm doing now. I just know I'm going to get faster and stronger every year. But I don't get too overly hung up on time. I think more about strategy and competing mentally.

"My strategy is to try not to plan out anything before the race. I look at it as a creative thing with many different elements—the people, the day, the weather, the course. A lot of it becomes very intuitive. You make the move without knowing why you made it, but it's the right move. I don't like to get set in any one strategy. I don't like always trying to follow or always trying to lead. I try to avoid being predictable.

"I respect everybody that I run against. But at the same time there is an ego thing where I believe I can beat anybody I run against. You have to. A lot of it is just saying okay, great, these guys are good, and they're going to run fast. There's really nothing to lose if I can stay with them or beat them. It's all sort of positive for me. Also, it is interesting going out and seeing what they look like, seeing how they feel, seeing that they hurt. The one thing that I always concentrate on is not letting anybody else win cheaply. If they're going to beat me, they can beat me, but they're not going to do it cheaply. At least they're going to hurt.

"I like to have a big fast pack. We've been talking about the competitive side of a marathon, and I think it's important to realize that everybody is competing against the race itself as well as one another. It's almost as if the race has a personality of its own. Everyone running under 2:20 is an ally you have to help along.

The marathon is a rival that I have ultimate respect for but ultimate aggressiveness toward. It's as if I have an appointment, an encounter, with it.

"One of the nice things is that, especially in running well or winning, there's an incredible sort of glow that lasts. It carries me through my training. It enables me to wake up in the morning feeling really tight or sore, and then motivate myself for another twenty-mile run just by flashing back to that elation of the race. It can last for months. Your mind blots out all the pain. It dwells on all the positive aspects. It's funny, too, because I really look forward to the two weeks before and the two weeks after, because I have to cut down on my training. It's like a forced vacation. Afterward my body is so wiped out. The whole idea of training becomes awesome almost, even running a mile.

"I don't agree that elite marathoners don't hurt as much as slower runners. I think that's something that three-hour marathoners have convinced themselves of, saying, 'those guys don't hurt and I do— they're superhuman.' Nobody has a monopoly on pain. It's how you look at pain and how you look at effort. You can learn to look at pain as an ally, as a means to an end, rather than an inhibiting thing. At Enschede I felt really good at the halfway point and took the lead and tried to push it. All of a sudden I got a very different kind of pain—sharp stomach cramps, side aches. It was like nothing that I'd ever felt, but I just fought it and decided that my conscious will was going to be stronger than that sort of involuntary pain. I said to myself this pain is just in the stomach, there's nothing really wrong, nothing's going to break or split open. This pain is just going to disappear if I concentrate on it and fight it. And the pain eased. I really believe that I overcame it. The body is always striving toward homeostasis, chemical balance and so forth, and when stress is applied it will find whatever way it can to eliminate that stress. I don't really believe in this split between mind and body because they're so interrelated, but in this case the body was finding a convenient test to say okay, the mind is driving me into this race. The body is sort of saying, okay, well, how

Joe Erskine, former boxer and crane operator, is a recent convert to running. He built these shelves just to accommodate his running shoes.

strong is the mind? How definite is it that it really wants to go through this? Will it put up with *this*? So it was a test and I tried to be conscious of it and fight it and say the mind is stronger.

"One of the more interesting things about running is the way you can achieve a state of mind and a degree of physical control that normal people never get to. With me the thought of running ten miles at a five-minute pace is usually just awesome. I know I'm running really hard when I achieve a six-minute pace in my training, and yet a marathon means twenty-six miles at a five-minute pace! And that's the result of the higher state you get into in a race. Football players make a catch and they don't even know how they did it—they just do it. Babe Ruth used to say how he could see a ball in slow motion and see the stitching on the baseball when it was being thrown at him at a hundred miles an hour. His mind was able to do those kinds of things. I think it's all there.

"One of the ways to get to this higher state is by stressing the body. That's the way in which the mind is taxed beyond normal limits and that's when these dizzying things start to occur. I don't really think there's that much difference between emotion or mind or physical exertion. It's all these things. There are really no words to describe it perfectly. It's concentration or excitement or intensity or just being high—but it occurs.

"Sometimes I'm amazed how many miles have passed. I go into this trance and boom! three miles have gone. It was just like nothing. Yet I have a very good awareness of time. I can tell to within a second what pace I'm running. So there's kind of a paradox here of being totally unaware but yet being very aware. It's like in meditation when you're supposed to dwell on your breathing and drop all thoughts. I think you get to the point where there isn't an awareness of anything. It's just awareness.

"The attitude of my parents has changed a bit in the last year. They never really believed that I could be any good on a world class. They always encouraged me, but I know now that they were concerned about my putting all this energy into something and having it so important to me when it didn't appear that I was ever going to be able to get any benefit from it in terms of achievement. I think it sort of amazes them. I guess they're proud. There's always the Protestant ethic. Like when are you going to get down and do something serious with your life. My mother would still like to see me practicing architecture or becoming a lawyer or something of that nature, which are all things I had considered doing.

"I think that most of the top runners go through the same kinds of experiences. Most guys don't want to talk about them or can't. Shorter is always putting down people who talk about running as therapy and that sort of stuff, but maybe he's gotten so bored at trying to explain it to nonrunners that it becomes a lot easier not to try. I think all the top guys are artists. They're all intense. That's what makes them tops."

In 1896 in Athens a Greek woman named Melpomene was refused official entry into the world's first marathon. She ran without a number and finished in about 4½ hours with a companion riding a bicycle alongside her. But for more than sixty years afterward women were kept from running marathons. The founders and bureaucrats of the Olympics, of sporting clubs and federations here and abroad, run by men for men, issued the standard litany of: too far, too much; women can't hold up; sports are unfeminine; long-distance running renders women sterile. Track events for women in Europe went up to 1,000 meters in length early in the century, and in the United States the longest AAU-sponsored race was 220 yards. Even women who were involved in physical education thought low-key participation, rather than intense competition, was the highest ideal for women athletes. Not until the early sixties did women in this country—in ones and twos—begin to infiltrate the hitherto-closed sanctum of road races and marathons. Some ludicrous but revealing scuffles took place. Nina Kuscsik, in an article on women's marathoning, noted that in 1961 a nineteen-year-old runner was told at the Manchester, Connecticut, road race that if she went through the finish line chute she would lose her

The beginning of the Bonne Bell race, for women only, in New York City in 1977.

amateur status. Two California women, Lyn Carmer and Merry Lepper, decided to run the 1963 Culver City marathon by hiding on the side of the road and jumping in at the start. Kuscsik wrote:

> A race official tried to push them off the road. Lyn punched him, asserting that she had every right to use the public streets for running. A sympathetic AAU official timed the women and Lyn went 20 miles while Merry finished the race in 3:37:07.

Roberta Gibb Bingay, a native of Massachusetts, bused out from California in 1966 to run the Boston Marathon. Her entry had been refused on the grounds that "women couldn't run that far because they would get hurt." She slipped out of some bushes near the start where she had been hiding and, wearing a beret, covered the distance in 3 hours and 21 minutes, finishing in the top third. The furor was tremendous, but Will Cloney and Jock Semple, race directors, refused to budge on allowing women to compete. In 1967 the notorious shoving incident took place along the Boston course. Katherine Switzer, whose application form read K. Switzer, was sent number 261 through the mail. Switzer, whose training had included a 29-mile run that spring, ran in a grubby gray sweat suit with a hood, accompanied by her coach and her boyfriend, Tom Miller. Cloney and Semple, who jumped off the press bus about 2 miles out to see what was going on, were both incensed, particularly Jock. Enraged, shouting he was going to get her out of the race as he ran up behind her, Jock was suddenly given an unexpected cross check on his left by Miller, a burly hammer thrower. Jock sailed off to the side of the road, gave up, and got back on the bus. Switzer, exhausted from the tension of the whole day, was bombarded by the press at the end. "One writer kept asking me if the reason I ran was to help the cause of women. I was so confused. I just wanted to run. I didn't want to prove anything. . . ." Switzer's finishing time was 4:30. Roberta Bingay, somehow less noticed in all the fuss, was running unofficially again and logged a 3:27.

The next month Maureen Wilton, a thirteen-year-old Canadian girl, set a new world record of 3:15:22. A New Zealand woman who had run a 3:18 in 1964 had held the best previous time.

In the late sixties and early seventies a small cadre of women marathoners, particularly in the United States and in Germany, thanks in part to Ernst van Aaken's helpful theoretical and coaching support, kept chipping away at official barriers and at the world's record. Improvement came quickly. Between 1970 and 1971 three American women, Beth Bonner, Sara Berman, and Cheryl Bridges, dropped the world's record four times from 3:02:53 down to 2:49:40. In 1972 the Boston Marathon finally took

Cindy Dalrymple: ranking woman marathon runner from Hawaii.

official women entrants. Ridiculous AAU regulations that were supposed to have the women's section starting ten minutes before the men at the 1972 New York marathon had been replaced in 1977 by a well-publicized AAU-sponsored international-class women's marathon in Atlanta, Georgia. The assemblage of the field, along with the presence of Van Aaken, focused attention on the reluctance of running's bureaucratic elders to establish a women's marathon in the 1980 Olympics. The International Olympic Committee and the International Amateur Athletic Federation have continued to keep women's distances in the Olympics at 1,500 meters.

One of the most remarkable and charismatic runners to emerge in the mid-seventies was Miki Gorman, a California housewife who at the age of thirty-eight set a new world record. She ran 2:46:36 in 1973 at Culver City. In October 1976 she ran the New York City Marathon at the age of forty-one in what is still one of the fastest women's times in the world—2:39:11. Born Michiko Suwa to Japanese parents living in China, she moved to Japan at nine with her mother and two younger twin brothers. Her father, a surgeon, remained in China until the end of the war. Miki, who moved to the United States in 1963 at the age of twenty-eight, still speaks English with a Japanese inflection. At times her inability to say what she means with the exact degree of precision she wants frustrates and embarrasses her slightly. But she has a keen ear for rhythms of speech and she vividly conveys the moods within herself and others—exultation, sadness, fatigue, coldness, and laughter. Within a few years of moving to the States she went out to Los Angeles from the East Coast, lived in a women's hostel, and worked as a secretary for a Japanese trading company. She met Mike Gorman, a stockbroker, at a dance, and six months later they were married. They have a bilingual daughter named Danielle, born early in 1975. The Gormans live in Los Angeles in a comfortable condominium-style apartment. Miki, who is only 5 feet tall and weighs 89 pounds, complains seriously about being too fat, but her appetite is happily unrestrained. Since she is near-

Miki Gorman, former world record holder for women in the marathon, at home in Los Angeles.

sighted she has trouble seeing her competition during races if they are too far away. She has no use for any of the vials of vitamins that Mike, a handball fanatic, has accumulated in a kitchen drawer. Although she was coached for a while by Laszlo Tabori, once an outstanding Hungarian middle-distance runner, she now trains without a coach.

"My husband likes to be active and I used to like to just be indoors. He started complaining! We knew this very athletic couple, and he said, 'I wish you could be the same way.' I tried weightlifting because I didn't like ladies conditioning. I like to do hard things. It's like a challenge. At first I didn't care for running when I started in spring of 1969. In October, the LA Athletic Club members run as much as they can. I ran five hundred and eighty-five miles. On the last day I tried to run one hundred miles, but I did only eighty-five. Since I didn't know anything about running, I didn't have any fear. I cried and cried when Mike said I didn't have enough time. And my legs were swollen and injured. For a whole month walking was difficult. The second time in October of 1970 I had total confidence. Mike was very encouraging and continually massaged me. I wasn't scared at all! I did a hundred miles in twenty-one hours. There were twenty starters and just two finished." Although Natalie Cullimore holds the women's American record of 16 hours and 11 minutes, 21 hours still represents a fine achievement. Only about two dozen people have run 100 miles in less than 20 hours in this country.

Another three years of steady jogging, covering 40 to 50 miles a week, went by. Then one day Peter Daland, the swim coach for the University of Southern California, came over to a surprised Miki Gorman and encouraged her to try some competitive running. Two close friends who became advisers and boosters from that time on were Lou Dosta, an aerospace engineer, and Dr. Myron Shapero, a general practitioner. She often ran part of her greatly increased training mileage that year, covering from 100 to 140 miles a week.

She finished her first marathon at Palos Verdes in 1973 in 3 hours and 25 minutes as an unofficial entrant. A week later, still exhausted, she entered her first official marathon and didn't finish. Six months later she ran her 2:46 for the new world record.

"I had no idea I was running so fast. I didn't know what I was doing. Actually Jacki Hansen* was in the race and I was afraid of her. I didn't think I could beat her. After about ten miles I closed up on her and she started to go faster. Oh, I thought, she's very fresh. At the thirteen-mile point, the turning point, she fell back. I smiled, but she wasn't smiling. I wasn't so competitive because I thought there was no way I could beat her. But during the race I built up more and more competitive feeling. After eighteen miles I was closing up on her again. I was going to pass her all of a sudden so I slowed down a little, took a rest, and stayed behind. Then I held my breath and sped up. After that I don't know how I did it. I ran fast, as fast as I could. I never looked back. There was an eighteen-year-old boy in the race, a Mexican boy named Carlos. Oh, I can never forget him. He thought I was a little girl! Around the ten-mile point we had started running together. He looked behind for me. Then Carlos slowed down and I never got to thank him, to say encouragement to him.

"Lou Dosta, who didn't finish the race, didn't see me crossing the line, and when he saw me, he said: 'What are you doing here?' 'I finished.' 'You finished? You finished! Oh, you've got the world record! Are you sure?' Oh, he hugged me! He was more excited than I was. That was a nice moment.

"I didn't get any local recognition. Yes, friends tell me what inspiration I am for them, give me very nice words, but the newspapers here are not like those on the East Coast. They didn't write up anything about me I think because I am Japanese. I remember two years before that I saw Cheryl Bridges break the world record at Culver City. She was beautiful—blond hair flapping and so skinny. Nice form. It inspired me, but I never thought I could do

---

* California marathoner, former world record holder with a 2:43:54 in 1974 and former American record holder with a 2:38:22.

Kathy Mills, #5001, and Brigit Seit, #1771, await the start of the 1978 L'eggs 10,000-meter race in Central Park, New York.

something like that. And the next day they wrote it up, and there was a beautiful picture in the newspaper, half page. And when Jacki broke the world record they wrote her up. And when I won Boston and New York—nothing, nothing! Finally once there was a little article.

"For the New York City Marathon in 1976 I had very good training. I trained too hard. Two weeks before I collapsed. I couldn't run any faster than a mile in eight minutes no matter how

Martha White and Aileen O'Conner are in with the lead pack at the start of the L'eggs Mini Marathon.

Martha White winning the L'eggs Mini Marathon in a record time.

I tried. I was angry at everyone. So grouchy! I thought running in New York would be impossible, ridiculous. At the race itself one man came up behind me and said: 'You're running 2:35.' And I said that's too fast. I got two times for twenty-one miles, but I didn't know which was really right. And it makes a big difference—maybe a chance for a world record. And I thought, is it possible? Can I do it? All kinds of thoughts were going through my mind. But I said to myself, well, I am so tired. I am ahead anyway. I can't break the world record. Should I slow down? On the other hand, I told myself no matter what time I get, if I don't do my very best I'll feel bad later. Don't worry about the record. Push yourself a little. I was aiming for 2:45 and I had a 2:39—I couldn't believe it. I could even cry now. I was so happy. It's so interesting, the joy of a marathon, such a quiet feeling, so satisfying. You want to enjoy the moment all by yourself.

"And after finishing interviews with the press I went to Barbizon-Plaza. I bought a can of beer. Oh, before that I called home. I could even visualize Mike jumping up and down. I was very quiet. 'Hi, Mike-san, I won.' 'You won? What was your time?' 'Two thirty-nine.' 'You're sure it's not 2:49?' I was very quiet. Then he yells: 'No kidding, Miksie, you did it! You did it!' He was so glad, so happy. I told him to call Lou and Myron. I went back to the hotel then and got in the bathtub. I put chamber music on. Then after my bath I lay down on my bed. There were beautiful flowers there. Tears came, I was so happy. So much satisfaction. I've *never* been so happy.

"At New York this year [1977] I raced against Kim Merritt.* She never talks. She's very competitive, but I like her. I think someday we'll be very friendly. She was very friendly at the Virginia ten-miler right after she had won the world record in the marathon. And she was winning all the races. She asked me: 'Miki, are you going to New York or Minnesota? I want to go where the competition is.' *I* want to go where Kim won't come. I saw her

---

* Wisconsin marathoner, current American record holder with a 2:37:57 in 1977.

Kim Merritt, one of the country's best women marathoners, pushes on under a hot sun. Women are running road races in ever greater numbers, and they still get a little extra support from the spectators.

and her husband in New York near my hotel. Someone I was with pointed them out, so I said, oh, and I crossed the street. I started talking to her, but she was very grouchy. She's so different from Virginia and I could tell that she did not have the confidence this time. She shows so easily how she feels. But I was afraid of her very much.

"At the start the women were all mixed in. I didn't know where she was. Before the mile point on the bridge I caught her and her husband running. I surprised her. I wasn't running fast on the uphill. 'Hi, Kim,' I say, 'you're going a slow pace today.' And I really meant it. Usually I don't see her at the beginning, but when I told everybody what I said after I got home, they said, ah, ah! what do you mean by what you said? They explained to me how it could be awful what I meant. I felt very bad. But she didn't answer. I ran one step ahead of her for six or seven miles. After seven miles she increased the pace and she passed me. Her husband and a friend were running on each side of her. I thought that she didn't look so good, a little heavy the way she was running. But I had never seen her so closely when running before, so I couldn't judge how she would do. I didn't know how I would feel at the end either so I just tried to concentrate on my own race. Then at twenty miles the crowd started telling me, 'First girl is about four hundred yards ahead.' Usually I don't pay attention because those distances aren't right, but many people kept saying it. Then three hundred yards. I thought they must be right. I got real excited. I squeezed my eyes to see better, and I saw blue and red and blond hair. And I thought, that's not a mirage, that's Kim! She was running slow, so tired. I daydreamed that I could catch her like Christa Vahlensieck caught her in the German marathon at the end, and it came to be real. I passed her the same way I passed Jacki—I held my breath. I looked back after a few minutes to see if she was behind me, but I didn't see her. I ran as fast as I could the last ten miles.

"Sometimes I think that I'm not anyone special, that anyone could do it. And then other times I think that I *am* special, I am

Toshiko D'Elia of New Jersey finishes a 1976 marathon.

different. I am very stubborn. I was brought up to be very patient and to endure. My father raised us with a lot of discipline. Packages in Japan come in a lot of wrapping all tightly wrapped in string. We couldn't use scissors to untie the knots. We had to do it with our fingers and unwrap very carefully, fold the paper and save the string. On train trips there were so many wonderful things, like ice cream and drinks, to buy, but I couldn't have any. Perhaps it was partly my father's concern for my digestion, which was very weak when I was a little girl. My mother insisted on putting into my lunchbox certain foods that I didn't like, and I had to eat them so that I got used to eating everything.

"Women runners ought not to have any secrets. They ought to share their training with one another so that everyone can improve. I can't understand why some women won't talk to me or smile for a month after I beat them in a race. Are men like that, too? Yes? But why do they do that? I have such respect, such admiration for people who beat me, I really do. Competitive running is a way to test yourself against others. Noncompetitive running is so special, so individual. Running is self-expression. It's like laughing and crying, things that you need to do."

6

Space Travel

The real solo artists, the crazies of the sport, all belong to that select and unnoticed fraternity known as ultramarathoners. They are the mammoth distance specialists, inspired lunatics who yearn to achieve mind-breaking feats like running nonstop through Death Valley or across the United States or around Hawaii or to dash through the 50-odd miles of a classic race, like the London-to-Brighton run, in times of 6 hours or less. They are the gnawers, the mental bulldogs whose motivation for clamping shut on the almost-impossible can sometimes try the understanding of family and friends. They do not stay at home much when they are in training. Some of them might be gone all day on a 40-mile training run. They might call from another city to tell you proudly what county they are in before they catch a train back. They plead to be let out of cars long before there are road signs announcing the destination. "I'll meet you later," they announce confidently. And they usually do. For in spite of their all-too-frequent aches and sprains, they are ridiculously healthy most of the time.

Not a great deal is known about this eclectic tribe, and although they possess the normal degree of human vanity, the world seems to ignore them almost entirely. The media's reaction—outside of the now-growing cluster of running newspapers—is total indifference. The general media has fixed on the marathon as the "supreme" and "ultimate" challenge. Ultrarunners merely smile when they hear such things. But what does it matter? Perhaps it keeps ultrarunning a bit more innocent. Not many other people really understand it. Cries of disbelief are gratifying to a point, but the best shop talk is always among fellow runners on the roadways.

The term *ultramarathon* simply refers to any race or run that extends beyond the length of a standard marathon. The usual untidiness of life makes it hard to define an ultrarunner other than to say that he is someone who does them—once in a while, often, or exclusively. They may frequently run marathons, but they may find them, in a commonly expressed lament, "too short," "too much of a pressure race." An ultrarunner is often a relative slow-poke who finds more room for achievement in the less cluttered spaces of 50-mile races, the most frequently contested distance in the United States beyond the marathon. Europeans gravitate toward round numbers as illogically as we do. They often have fields of over 1,000 for 100-kilometer runs. In the United States the national championships for the 50-miler, held some years on the West Coast and others on the East Coast, may draw from 30 to 50 entries, which for an ultramarathon is a big field. Women are beginning to appear more frequently in ultraraces, much as they did in marathons ten years ago, but the total numbers of contestants and races are still so small as to make large generalizations hazardous.

Ultrarunning is an odd sport in a way because it is as wild and chancy and tough to face up to as the uninitiated might imagine, and yet it isn't so very hard either. A great deal depends on how

Nick Marshall, an ultrarunner from Pennsylvania, douses himself with water during the Lake Waramaug run.

competitively it is run. There is no way to run 50 miles well, that is, near one's best, and not take a beating, not pay some kind of price for finishing. But it is possible to loaf along for a number of hours, have two sore feet and feel fine otherwise. But the time span is so long and the miles to be covered so many that the magic control of all the factors, all the variables, that runners so much yearn for, is simply not possible. Running in a heavy rain can be exhilarating in a training run, but for Ted Corbitt,* running in the dark after 22 hours on a quarter-mile track in England, such an unexpected downpour made the next two hours a nightmare. A slope that went unnoticed in the fast pace of the first 35 miles becomes a major obstacle to the hobbling effort of a runner who squandered his resources too recklessly. For that is the simple secret of successful ultrarunning—learning to gauge just how quickly to let one's energy flow. When the day's reserve is spent, there is nothing left by ordinary standards. One may then discover that the price for continuing when legs feel utterly wrenched and a weary mind feels grim about the whole enterprise is very high indeed.

Ultrarunners are not new. In the past, as today, some cultures have given great honor to ultrarunners. For the isolated present-day Tarahumara Indians in northern Mexico's Sierra Madre range, the winners of 150-mile kickball contests are highly respected. For the Tarahumara, running is more than a game—it is an important, quasireligious ritual that sometimes requires purification, special diets, the advice of shamans, and the healing aid of special powders and prayers.

In ancient Greece, specially trained couriers ran missions for cities and armies. Plutarch mentions Euchidas who ran from Plataial to fetch new fire from Delphoi—a round-trip run of 185 kilometers. At the finish of his run he fainted and died, a fate similar to Philippides'. To commemorate his run, he was buried in a sacred temple. Although it seems unlikely that a highly trained runner would die and not just collapse temporarily from exhaustion, hot weather and dehydration might have been a fatal combination. In the third century B.C., according to the historian Eusebius, a man named Ageus of Argos won the dolichos, or long race, in the 113th Olympiad and ran 100 kilometers (62+ miles) to his home to announce his victory the same day. Another runner carried news of

---

* New York City marathoner and ultramarathoner, American record holder for the 24-hour run—134.7 miles.

Frank Bozanich, a Marine stationed in San Diego, California, concentrates after a 50-mile race that he won earlier that day (1978).

the Olympic Games from Olympia to Epidaurus. This Drymas, the son of Theodoros of Epidaurus, legged 140 kilometers in one day and, like Ageus, had to cross the mountains of Arcadia. Pliny reports on messengers who ran between Sikyon and Elis—about 220 kilometers (about 137 miles)—in nine hours. Clearly no one could average 16 miles an hour over such a distance, but regardless of the actual elapsed time needed for such feats, they remain impressive.

The record of long runs since the Greeks is scanty. In his book *The Marathon*, John Hopkins mentions a run that may have taken place but almost certainly took much longer than the legend. A Norwegian runner named Mensen Ehenst ran round trip from Istanbul to Calcutta in 59 days, supposedly averaging 100 miles a day!

Ultrarunners are the Titans who extend the ordinarily accepted boundaries of human endurance. Ultrarunners teach us not only that much more is possible but that any remarkable feat of running is based on a complicated kind of simplicity. When Englishman Ron Hopcroft was asked how he set a world 100-mile road record of 12:18:16 in 1958, he said: "I just kept picking my feet up and putting them down until it was over." Similarly, the Tarahumara run without the benefit of shoes, formal training, or even what we would consider a minimally acceptable caloric intake—they average about 1,200 calories a day. The only conclusion one can draw is that human potential is far vaster than we care to recognize or ordinarily bother to explore.

For a time in the late nineteenth century, walkers who developed into runners were the ones who pushed the limits to a degree that has probably never been matched before or since. Ultrarunning has had cycles of growth and atrophy over the past one hundred years and will probably continue to have them. At present ultra-running is much like marathon running was years ago—unclut-tered, restricted to a few who know most of the faces at the handful of races and who have an unwritten sense of Spartan comradeship. Once you've been through one—well, it may not be undying intimacy or a relationship free from jealousy or competitiveness, but there are times when you talk about it with one another and you just know you have visited a similar space. The initiation scars are so subtly inflicted that one can only sense them.

Usually records are kept for ultradistance races on duly measured and sponsored courses, but occasionally ultrarunners indulge in solo runs that themselves are sometimes of a quasicompetitive nature, such as running across the United States for the "official" record. No one could possibly keep a complete record of every such venture. Besides, there is the problem of definition. Does a marathoner's 35-mile training run count? Does it matter at all? Of course, the answer is that it doesn't. But some solos seem without explanation to assume a special quality—they fit the quirkiness of the human mind, which loves large numbers and distances that fill in a gap between two well-known points, for example, the late Al Monteverdi's run between Milwaukee and Chicago, a distance of about 96 miles run in 14 hours and 50 minutes. Monteverdi was a race walker and a marathon runner with more than 125 marathons to his credit.

The transcontinental United States crossing, from New York to California or California to New York, has been one of the most "popular" mammoth runs, although the number of successful finishers is tiny. For a long time walkers were able to more or less match, if not better, running times. In 1928 the promoter C. C. Pyle staged a running contest from LA to New York in the hopes of making some money. First prize for the winner was $25,000, and the check went to Andy Payne, who then wisely retired. The second year The Bunion Derby, as it was dubbed by the press, went from New York to Los Angeles. Peter Gavuzzi, an Englishman, had put up a fine showing the first year by running in first place for 2,000 miles. The second year he returned he was again in strong position for first place. Gavuzzi's chief rival was the policeman Johnny Salo. Although they each had a car and a handler accompanying them there was help given to whichever one needed it. Gavuzzi even agreed to let his first-place margin of several hours slide enough to make for a more dramatic finish. He cut it too fine, and Salo's final burst after 79 days on the road brought him victory by a minute. Since Pyle had gone bankrupt, the runners never earned a cent for their labor.

In 1964 a tough fifty-four-year-old coal miner from South Africa named Don Shepherd made a solo crossing, covering 3,200 miles between LA and New York in 73 days and 8 hours. He found food, water, and lodging as he went along. He carried a few supplies in a knapsack.

In 1970 Bruce Tulloh, a talented English distance runner, did it somewhat differently. He got some sponsors to provide money and a car so that his wife and young son could accompany him and logged 2,876 miles between the City Hall in LA and the one in New York in 64 days 21 hours 50 minutes, slicing 8½ days off the previous crossing and averaging 44 miles a day. His book was called *Four Million Footsteps*, which referred to the approximate number of footsteps needed to propel him from start to finish. Tulloh read novels, poetry, and psychology at night during the trip, and he wrote with a certain eloquence about his state of mind and what such a feat really meant, if anything. His feeling when he reached New York, after so many days spent calculating mileage, how far he had to go, wondering whether he could hold up against the nagging injuries that sometimes plagued him, was one of relief. But even that, he said, "was tempered a little by a realization at the back of my mind that the game was over. Soon I would have to go back to the complicated world of responsibilities; from the simple round of run, eat, sleep and run I had to return to the problems of day to day choice . . . I feel on the physical side that the human body has far greater power of endurance and adaptability than most people give it credit for. I did that run without a day's ill health, without a day's rest and without any special diet or food supplement of any kind. . . .

"Then there is the matter of will. Whether you call it pride, self-importance, mind-over-matter or libido, there is a part of one's personality that carries the responsibility for pushing this thing through, and if it fails to dominate the body, then one will not succeed. It is a kind of overdrive that functions normally in cases of real need but is strengthened by adventures such as these. The danger is that this developing side of one's nature may cause an imbalance in the whole person, but the danger is decreased merely by being aware of it. My ego has fed on fame before; I hope that now it is sated."

Tulloh then goes on to note that, since he is at heart a Puritan, he has to ask himself whether "an entirely useless piece of physical endeavor" was worth all that expenditure of energy. And he says, because of what he learned and experienced, the answer is yes.

In 1977 a confident young Irishman from Queens, New York, Tom McGrath, trained through one of New York's most blistering summers, logging 30 to 50 miles a day. He set off from New York City with an Irish flag in one hand and an American flag in the other. One friend followed behind on a moped while his newlywed wife and another friend led the way in a borrowed camper vehicle. The three accompanied McGrath the entire distance—3,046 miles in 53 days and 7 minutes for a new record crossing. The chunky former Irish football player looked like a different man when he returned. The trip had taken its toll. McGrath lost a considerable amount of weight, and he had the look of a man who had been through an ordeal he would not quickly forget.

"It took me about three weeks to learn the rhythm of the run," he said. "When I woke up in the morning, I shuffled to the bathroom three inches at a time because the soles of my feet were so sore. Every day I wanted to stop, but I realized I had a commitment to fulfill and starting off with the flag you don't abuse that. I wore out eight pairs of shoes and had an injured arm when a passing truck brushed me. The only way to get through was to put one hundred percent concentration on the road and the road only. I was in such a state when I finished. I was king of the world then. But for about eight weeks after I finished I couldn't talk to anyone; I wasn't listening to a thing they said. I was jumpy, couldn't sit still. Finally I just told myself to come down."

Other point-to-point connections in the United States have drawn ultrarunners. Richard Innamorato, a New Yorker, decided he would like to take a look at all the coastlines in the various Eastern seaboard states. He rode up to Fort Kent, Maine, in 1975, found the northern terminus mile marker for U.S. 1, looked at it and started south. Seventy-two calendar days later (with only four nonrunning days) he ran up to the zero mile marker, having averaged 34 miles a day. "It was more like a vacation," he said. "I wasn't out to set a record. It was just an easy experience, not a pressure run." He covered the distance wearing a hip pack and for 1,500 miles was accompanied and aided by Peggy Fritsch, a girl friend, who rode her bicycle.

A now-forgotten boom of interest in ultras took place in New York City and London in the late 1880s. A handful of competitors called pedestrians pushed back the known limits of endurance under rigorous conditions in what were called six-day "go-as-you-please" contests.

These races are described in a monograph written by Tom Osler and Ed Dodd, two East Coast ultrarunners:

> The largest available hall would be rented for the contest and a track of from eight to perhaps 20 laps to the mile constructed. Starting on midnight Monday morning and continuing until midnight Saturday, the contestants would circle the track in an effort to log in the greatest possible mileage.
>
> The "pedestrians" . . . were free to run, walk, sleep, and eat at will, thus the term "go as you please." These were professional ventures and the victorious pedestrian enjoyed not only international notoriety but financial security as well. When public enthusiasm for these contests was at its peak in 1879, the winner could expect twenty to thirty thousand dollars for his week's work.

From 1874 to 1879 in both London and New York titanic duels raged between the great ones in the sport, but the real breakthrough came when the Englishman Charles Rowell introduced running into what had been a walker's struggle. In his late twenties, in the winter of 1882 at the old Madison Square Garden, Rowell set out to establish an unbreakable world record. An upset stomach forced him out of the race on the fifth day. In the meantime he set six world's records.

> 100 miles—13:26:30
> 200 miles—35:02:28
> 300 miles—58:17:06
> 24 hours—150 miles 395 yards
> 48 hours—258 miles 220 yards
> 72 hours—353 miles 220 yards

Osler and Dodd note that "only the 100 mile and 24 hour records have been bettered today. Rowell proved . . . that he was the greatest ultramarathoner of all time. Even today the world record for twenty-four hours is only eleven miles farther than Rowell's 1882 mark and Rowell faced another five days of running!"

In 1888, a few years before the final decline of these 144-hour marathons, the Englishman George Littlewood set the world's record of 623¾ miles at the Garden, a mark that still stands. He averaged almost 104 miles a day!

The English and the Commonwealth countries always seem to produce a steady trickle of ultrarunners, a few of them at almost any given time ranking among the top contenders and record holders in the world. Chris Stewart, a world-class middle-distance runner and marathoner, has speculated on why the English thrive at endurance feats. "The patience to keep on going under pressure is a British trait, I think. Britain endured two world wars, and under pressure the English dug their heels in. It's the same with a race. You go past them and they come up on you again. We don't really have any top sprinters. It's just not in our national temperament." One of the outstanding figures in the 1920s and 1930s was Arthur Newton, a British-born Rhodesian cotton and coffee farmer in the outback who began running when he was thirty-nine years old. He was hoping that by winning the annual 54-mile Comrades Marathon he could focus favorable publicity onto his failure to be compensated by the government when his farm was declared to be in a black area. He had never run before in his life. Newton never seemed put off by doing anything to which he put his mind. With his usual methodical approach he read up on what he could about the subject and on January 1, 1922, went out for a 2-mile run. On January 2 he desisted from running because he was "abominably stiff." Soon, however, progress was rapid, not to say extraordinary. A year and a half later he won the Comrades Marathon, coming from dead last in the pack to first. He won in 8 hours and 40 minutes. The following year he trained on the average 24 miles a day and won the Comrades again. Newton then decided to have a crack at Lloyd's amateur track record for 50 miles, which then stood at 6 hours 13 minutes 58 seconds. Newton ran solo on the Martizburg-Durban road, out and back on a hilly course, and sliced about 20 minutes off the record with a 5:53:05 performance, still a good time by today's standards.

In 1927 at the age of forty-five, Newton was encouraged by some friends in a running club he helped organize called the Bulwayo Harriers to take a try at the 100-mile record then held by an American named Hatch—a track time of 16 hours 7 minutes 43 seconds. As with the 50-miler, Newton decided to run his attempt on the roads, regardless of the rolling hills with "an occasional rise and descent of one hundred or two hundred feet." On July 12, 1927, Newton had a big breakfast at his hotel in Gwelo and started running in the predawn darkness. An official car puttered along behind, its headlamps on so he could see his way along the dirt surface. He ran the first 20 or 25 miles at about a 10-minute-per-mile pace "knowing I had to save every atom of energy lest I should fail from exhaustion."

"I had two or three drinks from a thermos between twenty-five and forty-five miles and was beginning to feel decidedly hungry and, between ourselves, somewhat tired, when we got to the hotel at Insiza, the halfway house, and welcomed the meal that had been ordered and was ready. My fodder was soup, chicken and vegetables, and fruit pie (pastry!) and I worked it back as quickly as I dared for no time must be wasted. Twelve minutes later I was out

A runner rests before the start of a 50-mile ultramarathon.

on the road again. . . . That meal certainly helped me along wonderfully and I felt the benefit of it for the next twenty miles. At about seventy, however, I knew that the real struggle was beginning. The sun went down and once more a car floodlighted the road while I crept steadily on, feeling that there was still a chance that I might reach the end, though I was in for a real bad time. . . . I found enough strength to potter along at about six and a half miles an hour, though every nerve and fiber seemed to be crying for rest."

Newton, though exhausted, finished in 14 hours and 43 minutes. The current record for 100 miles is held by English ultrarunner, Cavin Woodward, with a time of 11:38:54.

Newton's longest run came in 1931 at the age of forty-nine, when he took on a field of five other ultra men on a 12-laps-to-the-mile indoor track to try to set a new record for distance covered in 24 hours.

After he had raced over a hundred miles, Newton recalled:

"I daren't look at the big clock too often—I chanced it about once an hour—because I was getting very tired myself. But I knew that if I just kept up a gentle seven an hour or thereabouts I'd collar the coveted record all right. When you get really desperately tired you can't keep your mind off your condition; it won't answer to the helm as it does when you're fighting fit, and I remember thinking that never again would I dream of risking such punishing discomfort, though having already undergone so much, I'd have to battle through the few remaining hours. Even while this was passing through my mind I knew I had thought the same thing every time I'd had a really big race, and knew, too, that as soon as I had fully recovered from the effects I should be perfectly ready to have another and, hopefully, more successful 'go' at it.

"But I had only one job just then, and that was to travel along with the most perfect rhythm I was capable of; anything else and I might fail. . . . After all, it was only once in a lifetime and I had been working years to get to such a stage, so I'd just had to hang on no matter how tired I felt."

Newton did not fail. He set a new world record of 152 miles 540 yards in 24 hours. Two years later, already in his fifties, he made his fourth and final unsuccessful attempt to better the only record of his that made him feel dissatisfied, the 100-mile run. Bad weather and injuries foiled each try and, deciding that he was too old to hope for any more success, he left off serious competition. Newton's 24-hour run has been bested since but not by much. Forty-three-year-old Ron Bentley set the current world record on a quarter-mile track at Walton-on-Thames, England, of 161 miles and 545 yards.

Ted Corbitt, now fifty-nine years old, is a thin man with big feet, delicate hands, and a soft-spoken manner. Any solemnity on the part of an interviewer is dissolved by his wry humor, a kind of laissez faire attitude. During the day he wears medical whites in the fifth-floor gymnasium of NYC's Institute for the Crippled and Disabled, where he is chief physical therapist. His manner is so offhand and low key that even his staff don't know the extent of what he has done—that he was already thirty-two when he made the U.S. Olympic team in 1952, that he has run almost 200 marathons and ultramarathons, that he holds the American record for the 24-hour run, that he holds the second fastest 100-mile American performance, that over the years he ran nine 50-milers in under 6 hours each. His training runs have been fantastic endurance feats. His races have been marked by injuries, occasional shining wins, and some bitter disappointments. His name evokes an aura of tremendous mileage, of dogged persistence, unusual even among an unusual crew. Ted is unaffected, his surface manner unwittingly deceptive, showing no trace of the fiercely tempered spirit that sustained him through solo 100-mile training runs. He will talk if asked, but he never boasts, never shows sadness or regret, even though years of scar tissue and running in polluted city streets, and years of chronic injuries have brought his running to what has now become a long stretch of relative inactivity.

In 1950 Corbitt was thirty years old, still intrigued by what he had read about Tarzan Brown's win at the Boston Marathon four-

Ted Corbitt, the grand old man of ultrarunning in the United States, goes for a training run in his native New York.

teen years before. Ted had been a good runner in high school and at the University of Cincinnati where he ran 440 yards in under 50 seconds. Since college his training had been intermittent. Now he was really ready to see if he could prepare to run Boston. He turned to the scanty material on the library shelves and adopted some training ideas from Zatopek. Ted gradually increased his training load as he ran in combat boots through the streets of New York, hoping such heavy footgear would strengthen his legs. His first marathon time was a 2:48+, which was good for a fifteenth-place finish out of a field of 150. A chance meeting with Fred Wilt in Brooklyn's Prospect Park made a difference in Ted's plans. Wilt was the first runner Corbitt had ever seen out in the park, a far cry from the 1970s when the area is sprinkled morning and evening with joggers. Wilt, a 10,000-meter runner in the 1948 Olympics, encouraged Ted to try out for the 1952 Olympic marathon team. Ted qualified and went to Helsinki, where a sharp stitch in his right side dogged him the entire race. He finished forty-fourth with a 2:51:09.

Interwoven with the five or six marathons he ran every year were Ted's first tentative ventures—as they were for everyone in the late fifties and early sixties—into the world of ultramarathons.

Corbitt and marathoner Aldo Scandurra were among the handful in the New York area whose enthusiasm for ultras meant the revival of the sport in this country. The first Amateur-Athletic-Union-sponsored ultra was a 1959 Road Runners Club 30-mile run over a hilly course in the Bronx. Two years went by with no other ultraraces, but from 1962 on ultraraces became more frequent on both the West Coast and the East Coast. In 1966 the National AAU Long Distance and Road Racing Committee, with Scandurra as chairman, finally won support for a national championship run at the 50-mile distance.

Ted eventually ran the London-to-Brighton road race five times, never winning but taking second place three times. The 52.7-mile course starts at the foot of Big Ben as the clock chimes seven and finishes in sight of the sea in the town of Brighton. For his first assault he reviewed Arthur Newton's advice for successful ultra-running, but he resented Newton's comment that blacks had no ability to run long distances. Mixed in with Ted's other motivations was a determination to prove Newton wrong.

The number of marathons and ultras he took on increased as Ted got older. His two longest challenges were taken on in his late forties and early fifties. In 1969 he ran 400 laps on a quarter-mile track at Walton-on-Thames, England, where he took third place in 13:33:06. Four years later at the age of fifty-three, he took on a 24-hour run at the same track in England to set the still-current American record of 134.7 miles. He was third. What kept him at it for so long? What did he feel doing such things and how did he adjust to increasing age and struggle with chronic ailments?

"You do the things you have to do or want to do. Running is just something I did while growing up in South Carolina. I just kept it up and found more and more challenges in it. The same people that run marathons run ultras. The runners of ultras just train more. They put in more miles than marathoners need to. Certainly the ultramarathoner has to have the capacity to suffer longer. Why do I like the London-to-Brighton course? I'm not sure that I like it, but I ran it! I would describe the course as seductive. I wanted to see how well I could do it—it's the same appeal as a marathon. You have to prepare and train. After you work you want to cash in on it.

"You run slower in a fifty-miler than in a marathon. Around thirty-five miles is where it begins. Conversation disappears, evaporates. The monotony of pain in an ultra just doesn't let up. You've got a tiger by the tail. You've got people watching you. Each person has to deal with it on the basis of his own style. And you're getting chased, which is a reason to keep going, too. The only time I worry about the finish is if I'm injured. You always have in mind how much farther there is to go, but you're not dwelling on it. I'm generally relaxed before a run. Everyone tells you to relax, no one tells you how! On the London-to-Brighton course you have to stay alert to where you are because it's dangerous with all the traffic going on the two-lane road. There's no daydreaming as in training.

"For the twenty-four-hour race I was at a lower fitness level in '73 than in '69 when I first planned to run it. Mentally I was about the same. I ran over one hundred miles alone in one training run beforehand, which erased any fear I might have had or should have had. I was curious about it, but it was not like heading for an execution. I blotted out the prospect of failure. I remember the other runners were too nonchalant as a group. I knew they were worried. I had three hours of running comfortably. During the second hour I was on a tremendous high, the best running of my life. I don't know why. Then I started getting into trouble in the third hour. The pain in my thighs gradually came on, got worse, and finally stabilized. It just hurt to move. I kept hoping I would make a comeback, but the pain never eased up at all. It just got worse. Hoping for a break from the pain nourished me for a long time. But by seventeen hours I knew nothing would remove that."

In his book, *Corbitt*, John Chodes, a longtime friend and a handler for the 24-hour run, described the scene. The run had begun at six in the evening on a cool damp night with 15 competitors. Each runner's handler had a tent pitched alongside the track, with a cot and a portable stove in it. One large tent, illuminated by Coleman lanterns, housed the 15 timers who recorded each runner's lap. Chodes supplied Ted with Gookinaid, a commercial drink, every fifteen minutes. Other food offerings included two hard-boiled eggs crushed into a cup of orange juice, chocolate bars, slices of fruit, and blackberry juice. The first planned meal stop had been set for 100 miles but actually took place around 95 miles at eight in the morning. Ted walked a lap while eating a can of sardines. Although the handlers were initially competitive with one another and did not share information or refreshments, that "changed dramatically after seven hours, once the runners descended into the quagmire of fatigue and disability. Then friendship replaced rivalry. . . . All the handlers encouraged every man to prevent him from quitting. After the eighth hour victory and defeat lost their meaning. Survival was all anyone understood."

Four years later when asked whether the whole experience seemed like a dream, Corbitt answered softly: "It was a nightmare. It's real."

The margin of Corbitt's second-place position (which he had held for 13 hours) began to erode in the last hours. With 20 minutes to go as Corbitt slogged wearily along, Peter Hart, an Englishman, passed him by.

"After the heavy rains had come," Corbitt recalled, "I finally knew what the expression 'blow your mind' meant. The rain came so hard the curb on the track was obliterated. For the last three hours I ran in this and started to shiver. When I lost second place,

I didn't have to worry. I felt all right at the end, alert. I felt very stiff later. It probably took more out of me, left me with a physically deeper fatigue than I was aware of. In each of these races you've got to do your best because you can't go back. It's then or never. You haul yourself out forever."

Corbitt, who is convinced that runners don't take enough advantage of information already available about training, is a realist about getting older.

"With age you tend to lose strength. A lot of your juices are not as plentiful. There are ways to slow this process and counteract it to a point. Lifting weights will maintain strength to a very high level and stimulate some glands. Aging is an individual thing. And it means you have to change your goals.

"Why do I run? I've been running all my life. It's a kid's activity and I just never stopped it. There's always been the challenge of doing it, of trying to improve. The Olympics were just a way station."

One of the more potent names to emerge from the younger generation of ultrarunners in this country is Park Barner, who lives across the river from Harrisburg, Pennsylvania, in the small railroad town of Enola. Barner is a big guy with a powerful physique. Shy and reserved, he stands quietly among the chatting competitors before the start of an ultrarace. His eyes are what betray the intensity, the drive, the fire. Otherwise his manner is deceptive; his voice has a surprisingly high pitch. His thighs are thick and powerful and taper down along his calves to a startling thinness. He is indifferent to running chic's allure and has gone on training runs between cities in Bermuda shorts or run races in dark-colored socks. He expresses himself most fully once launched and running, becoming the bearer of a massive, seemingly inexhaustible fund of energy. Barner is no competitor to trifle with, despite his behemoth look and slightly ungainly running style. In the 100-kilometer Mechanicsburg race in 1975 he let a clubmate from the Harrisburg Area Road Runners Club, Al Somerville, surge far ahead of the pack. Somerville, who was wearing a see-through plastic bag from

Park Barner leads Don Choi during the 100-kilometer race at Lake Waramaug, Connecticut (1978).

the dry cleaners as protection against the day's wet snow and rain, blazed along for 45 miles. The upstart crown prince seemed to have seized the king's realm. Then, like a fisherman reeling in a fish barbed on fatigue, Barner began to close the gap. He said later in a typically low-key fashion that he wanted to run faster to warm up. He easily passed Somerville, who suffered bravely all the way to the finish. Barner set a new American record that day of 7:11:44. But he is far from invincible. He is a great runner, not because of his speed but because of his consistency, his immense and seemingly inexhaustible capacity to run slowly but easily for indefinite stretches of mileage. He has often run a marathon and a 50-mile race "back-to-back"—that is, one race on a Saturday and the other on a Sunday, usually having to travel to different cities to run both. Park definitely prefers longer distances.

"I can't talk in a marathon," he complains. "It's just about an all-out race for me, whereas a fifty seems like a training run because I can run slowly."

Barner, who at first startled his co-workers in Harrisburg by running in the building corridors on his lunch hour, says, "Nothing

Park Barner, his shirt stained with blood where it chafed his nipples, stands at rest after setting a new American record for 100 kilometers of 7:11:44.

specific got me going in running. Now it's just wanting to run farther and farther all the time. Ted [Corbitt] was an inspiration— knowing that he could do it. I would probably be able to run faster if I bothered with speed workouts, but it doesn't seem worth it just for a faster time. I like the notoriety, getting recognized, letting people know you can do it. I think that for the average person running an ultra is just too much to comprehend. It just sounds like it's impossible. It's funny because when I first started running, I had no idea people ran that far. There's no publicity."

Barner, who once considered turning pro as a bowler, gets tired, but he never seems to struggle to finish, never looks as if he has punished himself unduly. One of his runs that did cause a stir in the small world of cognoscenti was his 1976 approach to a 300-kilometer (186.4 miles) race along the C & O Canal towpath. It begins in Cumberland, Maryland, and ends near downtown Washington. The race until then had been run in three consecutive days in 100-kilometer legs, but Barner, for the sake of variety and challenge, decided to run the 187 miles straight through. It turned out not to be nonstop since he rested for 4½ hours, but, nevertheless, the total elapsed time was only 35½ hours.

Two friends, Al Somerville and Bob Crane, were Park's handlers, providing him with drinks, times, and encouragement. All the same there was no way to follow Barner directly since cars are not allowed on the towpath. Barner ran with a flashlight during the night and then narrowly escaped a bad bout with hypothermia, a disabling drop in core body temperature, brought on by running for so long in the nighttime cold of 18 degrees Fahrenheit. Later Barner recalled what happened.

"When I met Al at eighty-one miles, it really cooled off fast. It had been in the high forties the day of the race with a little bit of headwind. That night the wind died down and the temperature really took a dive. Just after it got dark I noticed frost on the leaves. Up till then I hadn't noticed it was that cold. When I met Al I put on an extra T-shirt and sweat pants. I thought that was all that I'd need. Because I wasn't running fast enough to generate heat, I guess my body lost heat all night. Finally about four o'clock in the morning it really hit me. I just had the feeling that I had to lie down and go to sleep, even though I was in the middle of nowhere. It was an almost overpowering feeling. I'd stop and bend over, but it really made me sleepier when I did that. When you run and get tired and you stop to take a break, it usually makes you feel better. In this case it just made me feel sleepier.

"The towpath was like a gravel road with tire tracks running through the sides and a little grass in the middle. It seemed like I was just falling asleep on my feet. Luckily I was getting close to where Bob and Al were going to meet me. It took me about twenty minutes to get there after I had this feeling.

"I knew the danger. I knew I had to keep going. . . . If I'd've laid down cold as I was and cold as the night was, that would have been it. I probably would have lost consciousness. They would have waited a half hour before running down the path to try to meet me. I hate to think of that.

"But anyway once I got in the car and they had the heater running I guess I napped for about a half hour. But after getting warmed up in the car I started shivering. I guess when you get so cold that you don't shiver, that's really bad. When I started running I felt like I was just starting out again. It was more the cold than the lack of sleep that stopped me."

One of the fastest ultrarunners in the country is Max White, light-haired and fair-complexioned, a comparatively youthful twenty-seven in a sport where runners can attain their best performances as late as their fifties. White, whose appetite for mileage is just as intense as Barner's, has a different attitude toward races. He won't enter ultras casually. He runs not just to finish pretty well but to compete, to win, to extract the best performance possible from himself. And he is wary of tapping too recklessly into his reserves. He likes conditions to be good. He fusses over variables he can't control, but once committed he is in to do battle. Heavy training has come easily to White, although he says he "learned things the hard way, through experience." Although as prone to tension as anyone else, White runs with an easy buoyancy and is one of the most relaxed and generous of running companions. He readily slows his pace to what is comfortable for everyone and somehow gives off a kind of sympathetic acceptance so that there is never any of that tacit stepping up of pace, the dueling between egos that can turn a training run into a racelike blitz. In 1973 at the age of twenty-two, Max blazed through the 52.7-mile London-to-Brighton course in 5:26:26, the fastest time over the course by an American. His 50-mile time was probably around 5:09, an unofficial best, although no times are given at that point on the course. A fair runner while an undergraduate at Princeton, he didn't begin to show his mettle until 1971 when he moved out onto the roads and started running marathons. He ran five of them in eleven weeks. He also ran some consecutive 200-mile-a-week training weeks, not really knowing much about training, just kind of figuring that a lot of mileage would help. As of early 1978 he had run about 26 standard marathons with a personal best of 2:20:40, five 50-milers, and a few other ultraraces. Ordinary training is 100 to 120 miles a week sandwiched in between teaching math at the Episcopal Academy in Alexandria, Virginia, and going over 150 miles a week during vacations. He runs interval workouts occasionally, works at stretching and weight training, and follows with his wife, Jennifer, an essentially vegetarian diet and uses no sugar, no salt, and no additives.

"I like to be comfortable for most of my races," Max says. "A couple of times a year I'll psych myself up for a supernormal race. But I run my best races when I'm relaxed. Before a long race I try not to get too keyed up and I try to keep a normal routine. Just before the race starts I'm breathing deeply, almost meditating, feeling a quiet anticipation, but I am relieved to get going. The last three days I walk around fairly gingerly. Every little ache or pain becomes amplified.

"A fifty-miler has a more reserved pace than a marathon. In a long race your perception of time goes more quickly when you're

Brian Jones of New York gets a congratulatory handshake after finishing fourth in the June 1978 100-mile run in Queens, New York. His time: 15 hours 8 minutes 2 seconds.

running with someone else, particularly the earlier stages when the competitive aspect is not in your mind. You just want to get through the first part in good shape. You go into a long race with some idea of what pace you can hold. But once I start running I just have a sense for the pace I should be going. My best race is going to be an even pace, and the longer the race the more significant that is. I have a feeling for the effort I can put out steadily over the race—whatever that translates into in terms of time, I'm content with.

"In a fifty-miler the race catches up with you. At a certain point you start feeling different. Between thirty and forty miles the complexion of the race changes. Sometimes you wonder if you will finish. Your thighs can start feeling very heavy. You know if you stopped you'd tighten up and you wouldn't be able to run anymore. I don't get fed up, though. I *want* to finish. I don't want to quit. You experience good patches and bad patches. I feel fatigued and then strong and powerful. I think the fluctuation is physical—the body's in a turbulent state. You hear voices. Your nerves are fairly shot. You have to tell yourself to keep moving your legs. You have to tell yourself to do things that you were doing automatically twenty miles earlier. You have to tell yourself to keep going, to stay tough. You have to remind yourself of how much training you've done for the race and that you know you can finish it. At times even the breathing isn't quite automatic either. Sometimes a license plate number I once saw—735 115—keeps repeating itself in my mind. On the last lap as the end is approaching, those images carry you along. It's magnetic. Your adrenaline regenerates. You are a lot more emotional at the end of a race. It's an unbelievable exhilaration to see the finish—the feeling a discoverer would have when he discovered an island. It's kind of a shock to stop. I feel tight in my diaphragm. The race can kind of hit you all of a sudden. And you stiffen up. You literally can't run anymore after hanging around a few minutes. And then there's a period when I start really fading. If I'm dehydrated I feel very much removed from life—almost like I was dying."

It isn't easy for some people to believe that such extreme ventures don't always mean unbelievable pain and discomfort. But to a trained distance runner, most of the running is more than comfortable, it is pleasurable. Pleasure is a funny word, though. One may feel at times, on a long training run, an increase in self-awareness and in the clarity of one's thoughts. This feels good. The stretching out of body capacity brings pleasure because it calls for just enough work and effort to require a concentrated response. And also the more one runs the easier running gets. It is the race itself, not the running, that cuts the skin and splinters emotional bones, but that happens only a few times a year.

A training run of staggering dimensions feels sweetly gritty. Everything has happened on it. You go out in darkness and return home in late afternoon light. The world has gone on, waking up, driving, venturing here and there, while you have cut through like a knife, composed, self-driven, blessed by the illusion of perpetual motion. All the choices that might have been, all the options for not doing it, are bypassed, so that at the end you peel off your socks and feel a special rest that goes beyond the animal satisfaction of stopping. The day has been consumed by will. There is nothing left to show for it. How was your run, they will ask you when you return from 50 miles, and you try to avoid saying something and go on saying too much, but who cares? Who can feel what you felt? One is saturated with the odor of change and mystery, but it cannot be given directly to others. Isn't it dangerous? they ask. Isn't it too much? How can you put so much time in? Why don't you grow up? They react to the idea of it, not to what it was. Such runs have private meaning. They are rewards. Or pieces of luck.

One day Max White set out on a run from his home in Charlottesville to Richmond, 75 miles distant, where his parents lived.

"It was just a natural stretch," he said. "It was kind of tempting. It wasn't as if I was running into oblivion. Jennifer and I were headed over to the track for a morning run, and all of a sudden the idea of doing it flashed into my head. I said: 'Jen, I'm running to Richmond this morning.' She said: 'What? You got to be kidding.' I said: 'I'm running to Richmond.' She said: 'You just can't run to Richmond. That's something that you have to plan for.' I said: 'There's no way that anyone would ever plan to run to Richmond.' It's just the kind of thing you have to do a little bit on impulse, so this was with no planning.

"I took off for Richmond on Route 250, which was the old road to there. Jennifer had had time to take her run and go home, shower, and go to church. Then she called back to see if I had changed my mind. There was no answer. Then she took off. About forty-five miles after I had started out Jennifer came up behind me in the VW and she started giving me ERG. I was fairly dehydrated by that point. For the next twenty miles I must have gone through a gallon of it. It wasn't causing me any problem at all. It was just soaking right in. I think that had something to do with my picking up the pace. She'd drive five miles ahead and give me some more.

"I do remember being more emotional during the last part of that run. People were giving me a hard time in Richmond. People were yelling from some of the cars, 'Hey, jogger!' One car swerved in front of me. I was really mad and gave him an unpleasant gesture, and then after he had had his charbroiled burger, he came whizzing back yelling obscenities. Then I realized that I had no reason to gesture at him even if he had cut me off, so I started waving at him. I said: 'No problem, I'm not mad at you.' He's still yelling obscenities at me! I thought it was a little bit ironic. Here I'd run seventy-four miles and someone in a car was giving me a hard time. I remember at about a mile and a half to go Jennifer had talked about driving way ahead and stopping at the store, and I didn't want her to leave. I wanted her to stay close by. Very emotional. Maybe a little bit worried. But it was not nearly as intense as if it had been a race.

"We walked in and told my parents what I'd done. My mother was upset. Here I was anticipating a warm greeting. She said: 'You fool!' or something like that. 'That was a stupid thing to do.' I remembered things I wish I could have conveyed to her at that point about positive reinforcement and making someone feel wanted. My father's reaction was similar. In a way I'm glad that Jen hadn't called them up beforehand because then they might have wanted me to stop. The next day I went out running. I wasn't all that knocked out."

One of the most freewheeling of spirits is Don Choi, a thirty-year-old postman who covers his route in San Francisco by running it with his 35-pound mailman's sack slung over one shoulder. He is proud of being a postman, proud of doing a good job and covering his territory faster than anyone else. Both parents are from mainland China and Don talks English with a slight accent. He listens carefully to questions, pauses, and then says, "Yeah," thoughtfully, not ducking, trying to give the best answer he can.

Don Choi finishes fifth at Lake Waramaug (1978).

His humor is zany and he can burst suddenly into a rising crescendo of laughter that pulls his listeners along with him. When he describes himself as impulsive, it is easy to believe him. He exudes tremendous, unaffected relish for his avocation of drawing the most from himself—and not just in running. For a while during 1977 he was running his postal route, running about three hours a day in addition to that and working out after supper on an indoor skiing machine until a sudden injury from too much stress meant he couldn't run the 50-mile championship in Santa Monica. Race day was one of the saddest days of his life. He cried, he says quietly, not asking for sympathy, simply reflecting on the oddity of being slapped so hard by life when he was only trying to ready himself for a joyful enterprise. Skiing, mountain climbing, cycling—all are sports that have drawn his fancy.

"My father influenced me a lot. He came over on his own from mainland China when he was very young. He used to fly airplanes out of O'Hare Airport in Chicago back in the twenties. There's a picture of him in the open cockpit of a biplane, wearing goggles and thick overalls. He taught himself English, had a job, played for various teams, very busy guy. In high school he wanted me to become a gentleman-scholar-athlete, but I played basketball. It drove him crazy when I came home with a concussion or a broken ankle.

"I used to play a lot of table tennis until I saw the Munich Olympics on TV. Running was poetic. It required dedication and I wanted to try it. My life didn't have as much meaning as it could have. I just do things on impulse. I ran my first ultra for that reason.

"A fifty is shorter than a one hundred, that's the difference! You don't slow down as much in a fifty. A one-hundred-miler is a very drawn-out affair. There's not much difference between ninety and one hundred miles. Of course at one hundred, you're elated. I even got a second wind then—must have been my finishing kick. Once you get over eighty or ninety miles, it's just a blur, you're so numb. You just push yourself. I consider the fifty a speed race.

"I'm getting away more and more from competitiveness. I'm

getting more into a personal expression of running by going for one hundred miles or twenty-four hours. What do I mean? I'm doing it more for myself. I knew from when I was very young that I had a capacity for endurance in anything I do. It's just finding the limits. I found those limits in the one-hundred-miler.

"But Lake Tahoe* was my high point, my best experience in running. That's because I gave everything, physically and psychologically. When I got to the sixty-five-mile mark I knew I was way ahead of everybody, but I was dying. But I said, I'm not going to slow down. Images would come up of people who'd influenced me in the past, people who meant very much to me throughout my life. I said, okay, I'm doing it for them. They probably won't know a thing about this, but I know, so I really gave it all I had. When I finished, I was sky high for three weeks. Not many things can come close to that.

"I'm hoping for that same kind of exhilaration when I try these other things. But this Death Valley thing is going to be a long run. To get out of the Valley I'll have a five-thousand-foot climb. Once I reach Mount Whitney I'll have run in excess of one hundred twenty miles. After that will come the real test of willpower. I can't say what's going to happen, what it's going to take, what I will have left at that point. And I'll be glad to reach the foothills, even to get up a mile of Mount Whitney. If I don't reach the top, well, I can always try it again sometime.

"Willpower means certain things to certain people. For me, it's very simple. It's mind, and if your mind wants to do it, your body will do it. If you think it's impossible, then your body won't respond to it. People ask if I get bored running one hundred sixteen times around in that one-hundred-mile race, and I say, no, I don't, because I concentrate on the body. The mind is saying loosen up the elbows, this is getting stiff. You're constantly thinking, but in

---

* Choi won the 72-mile-long run around Lake Tahoe on the California-Nevada border the first year it was held in 1976 with a 9:45:14. The course is over 6,000 feet in elevation.

a fifty-miler you also have to think about your competition. That's why I don't enjoy it—it's so short a time. I'm getting into looser things. A lot of people say, gee, you're really competitive. I say, no, I'm expressing myself, and this is the way that I do it. It may sound crazy to you and you might not understand it, but this is where I attain my highest levels of whatchamacallit.

"When I was eight years old, I was always asking my brothers and sisters, you may know me, you know my name, but do you really know me inside, and they would say, you're crazy, your

After a 100-mile race is over, the weariness really shows.

name is Don Choi, we see you sitting right here in the kitchen. Well, you may see me, but do you know what I'm thinking, do you know who I am? I was always questioning myself, trying to reaffirm my existence and what I'm trying to do in running is to reaffirm my existence. Maybe I'm totally insecure or something, I don't know, but I have a lot of fun.

"I think you have to have a very strong psychological makeup to run ultras. You have to have very solid resolutions about yourself. Yet I think if you want to get into long stuff, you have to be relaxed. Try to enjoy it and you'll get the most out of it. You'll appreciate yourself a lot more. You'll find out things about yourself. Once it's over and you *know* you gave yourself to it totally, you feel elated. But whatever I do in running, it will not compensate for shortcomings in other areas. How do I explain that? I can't. I don't go around telling everybody that I'm a runner. A lot of people on the route don't know that I run, or they think I'm a jogger. I know that if I say 'a hundred miles,' they won't comprehend well. When I run, I concentrate on my running. When I deliver my mail, I deliver my mail. But I don't go around and say—it would be socially awkward—look, look what I've done. You don't wear a badge saying Death Valley to Mount Whitney. I don't fool myself with that. Nobody's perfect. I have problems. In a way certain problems do get resolved in the running, but running is something for me to enjoy. Sometimes it disturbs me when other people say, you're a runner. Then they categorize me. It's very difficult to discuss ultramarathons with runners as well as with the general public. A lot of times I'd just rather not talk about ultras.

"Ultramarathoners are a varied group. Some of them are intensely competitive, and they get aggravated with certain things. They're absolute perfectionists, and when the run is over, I kind of feel sorry for them because they don't get out of it what I got out of it. I'm still learning about different ways of enjoying ultramarathoning."

7

Running
Your First Marathon

For many long-distance runners, joggers, and dreamers, the ultimate test is to run the marathon. Perhaps never having run one yourself you are wondering if you can do it too, or if it is a feat beyond your capacity. The number who want to find out continues to grow fantastically. In 1973 the New York City Marathon drew about 300 entrants, in 1977 over 4,000. The marathon was once the preserve of the dedicated male oddball. Now it has been taken up by women, children, the handicapped, the aged, heart attack victims—many of them people who never bothered with a sport before or thought themselves capable of more than a dash after a runaway dime.

Set modest daily goals to achieve an immodest and difficult task. Heroics without experience or adequate training will lead to a DNF, a "did-not-finish." Aim for finishing your first marathon and be happy with a time that reflects a relatively steady, if slow, pace. To run a marathon is to fight a battle of attrition. That experience, whether easier or harder than expected, is impossible to ever completely predict. Both training and racing happen one step at a time. This chapter, meant for both the rank beginner and the person already running, can mention only the basic elements in a training program. These are general guidelines gleaned from my own and other people's experiences, which you will have to explore and then tailor to your own needs. For more detailed sources of information and reading, consult the list at the end of the chapter and ask other runners you meet for advice. Unfortunately, advice can get confusing. Everyone has different theories. Runners follow some rules and break others with impunity. The main hazard to avoid is rigidly tailoring your own physical and mental needs to someone else's training program. You will find yourself your own best guide. There's some struggle in building up to higher levels of fitness, but basically training should not hurt. And eventually, as discomfort for the running novice fades, it ought to be fun. If you don't enjoy running, you'll find dropping out irresistible. And that would be a pity.

It helps to understand why you want to run a marathon. Running it for yourself will make training and the actual race a lot more enjoyable. It's not worth doing just because the fanatics you run with pressure you to try one or because you think it will make you a "real" runner. In many ways the marathon has won its glamour at the expense of interest in shorter road races. It happens to be the longest standard-length race accessible to almost anyone who can put in the necessary training. It also happens, by chance, to be 26 miles and 385 yards long. Few hear about or care to try the ultramarathons of 50 and 100 miles. Those races require heavy mileage background and a devotion to running that few are willing to bother to maintain. And even those "ultimate" races turn out to be relative to even longer ones. The point is that there's no reason to feel guilty "just" running, say, 3-to-5-mile races. They are just as much fun, are widely held, and require far less recovery time than a marathon. To do well over a 5-mile course requires all the intensity, personal struggle, drama, intelligent planning, and excitement anyone could wish for. If you're happy where you are, fine. Otherwise, there's every reason for giving into the lure of the marathon. It is a demanding race and there is ample testimony from many runners about the intense personal rewards found in taking on that challenge.

Dr. Kenneth Cooper, author of *Aerobics*, recommends that those getting started in a fitness program should have a history and a physical examination within the preceding twelve months if they are under thirty. Those thirty to forty years of age should have a history and physical, and a resting electrocardiogram (EKG) within the previous six months. The ideal for anyone over forty would be a history, a physical, and a resting and stress EKG within the previous three months. Dr. Cooper also believes the safest way to build up is slowly and progressively. The latter point cannot be stressed too much. Many who start an intensive running program get injured or overtired or discouraged by not seeing their unrealistic expectations met. Finding a balance between timidity and laziness and foolhardiness is not always so simple. Learning to handle a greatly increased running program requires much more than just getting yourself out the door, running for "x" miles, and then coming back and forgetting it. It requires common sense and careful monitoring of internal attitudes and body responses.

The basic theme of preparation is to build up your aerobic base, your body's ability to sustain continuous running over a long period of time without going into oxygen debt, a state that can be only briefly sustained. Although it's good to vary the pace by going faster when you're able, 95 percent of your mileage ought to be aerobic. When you're running out of breath, you're running too fast. You ought to be able to talk and run at the same time.

The minimum amount of training necessary to run a marathon is a weekly average of 45 to 55 miles for two to three months immediately prior to the race. Clearly, there is some flexibility in that range. Although it is not as effective as training a minimum

At the first annual Empire State Building Run-up, Marcy Schwam waits under the glare of TV lights before the contestants assemble.

of 65 miles a week over the same period, it is sufficient. Multiplying your daily average of miles run in training times three gives your approximate maximum comfortable limit in a race. It just happens to be a useful rule of thumb. That doesn't mean that you will feel comfortable the whole way through. It means you can run up to that distance relatively hard and be trained to withstand it. If your daily average is, say, 7 miles, you can reasonably expect to find that after about 21 miles into the marathon the mental and physical struggle to finish will greatly intensify. Running a daily average of 9 miles means that the last 5 miles may also be hard to complete, but that the degree of erosion will be somewhat diminished. It isn't possible to talk about the number of training miles run as a precise indicator of race performance, because too many other factors come into play: pace, weather, age, previous fitness level, inherited physiological characteristics, and so on. Some of these will be considered shortly.

You'll have to find a schedule and a level of training that suits you best. Running a minimum of five days a week (hopefully seven) will bring steady improvement. If you have never run before at all on a regular basis and even the shortest jog leaves you winded, begin by walking. Dr. George Sheehan, a New Jersey physician who has become one of running's most respected medical experts, suggests using a "scout pace" if necessary (alternating fifty steps walking with fifty steps running). Eventually your continuous running will increase to about thirty minutes, a comfortable plateau, which Sheehan terms "the endpoint for fitness. That 30 minutes will get us fit and put us in the 95 percentile for cardiopulmonary endurance. At 12 calories per minute, it will eventually bring our weight down to desired levels. It will also slow the pulse and drop the blood pressure. It will make us good animals." How far you go from day to day will vary as will the speed at which you run, but those variations don't matter at first. What matters at this stage is running for the thirty minutes without strain. If you can talk and run at the same time, you are going about the right pace.

If, for you as a beginner, this thirty minutes a day takes some working up to, keep your goals high but your training increments modest. A 15 to 20 percent increase in total monthly mileage allows the body plenty of time to adapt to the increased work load. If you want to take longer in increasing your mileage up to 45 to 55 miles a week, do so. It is always better to err on the side of being too conservative. Greed is the cause of many running injuries. As time goes by, your knowledge of and sensitivity to bodily clues will deepen in sophistication. As likely as not, days will come when you are just plain tired. There are many signs of the onset of fatigue that can be ignored or suppressed for a while, but it will eventually claim its payment—rest, whether enforced or voluntary. Rest is a dirty word among runners. The stubbornness needed to run a marathon can be a hindrance, too. It can be extremely dif-

Two teammates exchange an embrace at the end of a hard run.

ficult to enter "zero" miles for the day in your logbook. The tyranny of numbers and ambition can lead to an overly rigid schedule. Neither you nor your body is a machine. It's a mystery grappling with a stubbornly recalcitrant body or state of mind. It may require one or two days of diminished mileage, or complete rest. The shocks and cumulative strain of distance running, especially on hard surfaces, are not what the human body was designed to take. Appreciate your body's needs and it will do wonders. Deepening fatigue can be marked by some or all of the following: irritability; sudden, unexplained drops in performance; insomnia; loss of appetite; change in bowel habits; nagging, persistent aches and soreness; and lack of zest about the daily run. Without rest these symptoms will continue and worsen. When you're tired, resistance to disease drops and muscles and tendons are more likely to give out.

Once your mileage is up into the forties it helps to acclimatize the body to the stress of a marathon by setting aside one day a week for a longish run, perhaps two to three times as long as your daily average at that point. At the start, take these runs nice and slow and incorporate as many walking breaks as you need until you can complete a given distance without needing them. Then gradually increase the length of your long training run. A minimum of three long runs of 15 to 18 miles in the two months before your first marathon would be a useful precaution. Although it isn't necessary to have run a 26-mile training run beforehand, these longer runs have several benefits. They will increase your confidence about handling the marathon distance, and get your body used to the feeling of being on the road for at least two consecutive hours. It will also further develop your sense of pacing. A marathoner, even the best, has a limited supply of energy. The trick is to gauge how quickly you expend it—too fast a pace early on can bring a dramatic slowdown in the latter stages of the race.

It's also useful to have run some short races before racing a marathon. The longer the race, the longer recovery takes. A 5-mile run on a Sunday may mean a couple of days of very easy running before you feel fresh again. A 20-mile race will take longer than that. The basic principle in your first races should be the same as in your first marathon. Run slower than you would like the first half, at a hard but still comfortable effort. When you reach the halfway point, try to maintain the same speed all the way through, or run at a faster pace if you can. These shorter races provide a welcome change from the unbroken round of steady and moderate-to-slow running. They sharpen muscle coordination and keep you from becoming psychologically stale. And these shorter races teach a sense of pace under stress conditions when it is so easy to misjudge how fast you're going. The novelty of the crowded start and the jostling after the gun goes off, the dynamics of your own reactions and those of others during a race, the friendly comments, the stringing out of the pack, your isolation when the group behind is too slow and the group ahead too fast to catch, the runners who surge forward during the later stages and those who slow down, panting and struggling—all these experiences become familiar and thus add to your confidence. The greatest fear can come from simply not knowing what to expect. Short races provide useful approximations in miniature of the marathon experience.

Training almost always brings problems. It would be nice to pretend that running was an instant, effortless road to fitness, but it isn't. Nevertheless, almost all of the problems that come up can usually be resolved and often prevented. Prevention is a dull topic because you can't always measure its benefits—until you ignore it.

Of prime concern is the care of your feet. Some people can get by running in tennis sneakers, army boots, and bare feet, but for most of us, it is advisable to get a good pair of running shoes. Why?

"Shoes are for protection, support, traction, cushioning from the ground, balance of foot deformities and the accommodation of foot injuries," answers Dr. Harry Hlavac, chief podiatrist at the Sports Clinic in San Francisco. "A proper shoe should provide support and cupping of the heel, firm arch support, protection of the ball of the foot, and flexibility of the front sole for easy push-off."

Running shoes fall into two general categories: racing flats (extremely light, thin-soled, and with minimal cushioning) and training flats (medium to heavy weight with thick soles and adequate cushioning). Training shoes, as their name clearly states, are designed to provide protection for your feet during the ordinary day-to-day drubbing of training. They can, however, be used for racing. Their chief disadvantage compared to racing flats is their weight. It means carrying an extra two ounces or more of weight per foot. Considering that you make 40,000 separate foot strikes in the course of a 26-mile run, that can add up to a lot of extra weight. However, the racing shoes provide far less support than your feet have become accustomed to and the additional soreness, impact shock, blisters, etc., can balance out the advantage of speed. Which kind you choose for a race is an individual matter.

Be sure you get a good fit. Look for shoes that are snug but don't pinch, especially around the toes. Check the fit standing up rather than sitting down. If your feet are too wide or too narrow to be comfortable in reputable shoe brands like Adidas, Tiger, Nike, Karhu, Brooks, Pony, Converse, Puma, or Etonic, then try New Balance models that provide variable shoe widths. The front part of the sole (under the ball) should be flexible, not stiff. Look for a well-built-up heel (up to an inch thick), adequate cushioning along the sole, and a heel counter (cup around the heel) that is firm and snug. The shank of the shoe (under the arch) should have a full width, because that is where your foot most needs support if it is landing with any kind of abnormal motion.

According to Joe Henderson, former managing editor of *Runner's World*, nearly all running injuries are self-inflicted. They result from going too long or too fast, or from a combination of the two. He suggests a slow start to the daily run, particularly in the morning when the chance of injury owing to physical stiffness is greater. Stopping in the middle of a run to stretch out tight calves or hamstrings also offers protection against injury. Running, for all its benefits, tightens and shortens the lower back and leg muscles; it also makes the posterior muscles far stronger than the opposing ones. This imbalance increases the risk of muscle strains, pulls, or tears. Stretching exercises should be done both before and after a run. They can include yoga asanas such as the back stand or the plough, or any other flexibility exercises (such as dance warmups) that provide a gentle but thorough stretching out. Of particular help to runners with tight calves are wall pushups: place both hands on a wall and lean into it with your feet about six to ten inches away. Bend one knee to increase the stretch in the opposite leg. Bent-leg situps to strengthen stomach muscles are also of considerable importance.

When a program of stretching and strengthening does not seem to help a persistent, disruptive pain, it could well be time to visit a podiatrist. If the foundation is weak, the whole house may tilt. A significant number of runners have a variety of imbalances in the way their feet strike the ground. One leg is often longer than another. A runner may have an unusual amount of bowing in his leg bones, or a combination of similar factors that leads to pain not just in the feet but in the shins, the knees, the hamstrings, the sciatic nerve, or elsewhere. Dr. Richard Schuster, a Queens podiatrist who has been a pioneer in the treatment of runners, decries their tendency to be too stubborn.

"I think it's a crazy habit to ignore pain," he says. "I think you should try to run through annoyance, but don't run through pain. Pain is destruction."

Dr. Schuster feels runners can make certain kinds of preliminary self-diagnoses of actual or potential problems.

"Shoe wear is a good indication of when you should be suspicious. Shoes seldom wear evenly. The average shoe wears a little bit on the outside of the heel and maybe a little bit on the outside of the ball. But if you have any concentrated areas of shoe wear— under the middle of the ball or at the end of the first toe or to the point where it grinds through into the subsole—anything that is accentuated or exaggerated—this is good reason to suspect an imbalance.

"There is a simple way to detect imbalances in your own feet. You can't do it yourself, but someone else can help you. Take shoes and socks off, kneel on a chair and relax. If the heel lines up with the leg, that's fine. The ball should be parallel to the heel.

But where the ball is inverted and does not line up with the heel, you've got an imbalance. You can see that very easily just by sighting down the foot.

"One imbalance you can't find that way is the one that might occur in the upper leg, in the tibia. But you can be pretty suspicious of a leg imbalance by standing and looking at your shinbones. If they come in as commas or parentheses, there might be an imbalance. However, this test is not one hundred percent accurate.

"The three basic areas of imbalance are the forefoot, the rearfoot, and the leg. The cause of them is usually a retention of the prenatal position. Before you're born, you're rolled up in a ball; everything's been turned in. By the time you're five or six all of these things should have straightened out, though this doesn't always happen."

Sports podiatrists like Dr. Schuster often treat runners by providing them with leather or acrylic inserts to be worn in their running shoes, or they may simply prescribe certain stretching and strengthening exercises. Make sure the podiatrist or orthopedist you go to is familiar with treating runner's ailments. Rest and cortisone injections (which can cause damage to connective tissue) are an old line of treatment not worth paying for. And it never helps the underlying problem. A podiatrist familiar with the special stresses of running finds a way to treat the cause as well as the symptoms. Any disturbing foot, knee, leg, buttock, or lower-back pain is worth a trip to a podiatrist to avoid serious trouble later on. What is mildly annoying at 30 miles a week can be impossible to put up with at 60 miles a week. Remember, though, that shoe wear beyond a quarter of an inch can sometimes cause a variety of pains. Keep your shoe heels built up with commercial compounds or glue applied with an electric glue gun. When home repairs fail, get them resoled. Running shoes are too expensive to buy casually, but if they get worn beyond repair and comfort, throw them away!

Weather presents special but easily handled problems. Cold weather is the easiest to dress for. The body loses the most heat through the scalp and the hands. Cap and gloves do wonders for making a chilly day seem tolerable, even in shorts and a T-shirt.

Three friends congratulate one another after finishing the January 1977 Asbury Park, New Jersey, marathon. Freezing temperatures, icy footing, and heavy snowfall made it a miserable day for running.

Several light layers of clothing are better than one bulky sweater. Not until the wind-chill factor gets down to around −40 degrees Fahrenheit do you need to worry about freezing air damaging your lungs. Thermal underwear is one of the lightest and most efficient running garbs a fanatic can get decked up in—however, be prepared for some sniggers. On extremely cold days run against the wind at the start and with it on the way back.

Heat presents far more danger than cold. It is not easy to avoid overheating. Once the temperature rises above 85 degrees Fahrenheit and the humidity pushes the temperature-humidity index (THI) above 75, special caution is required. Overexertion on a hot day for the nonacclimatized runner can bring on heat exhaustion, heatstroke, and even, in a few cases, death. Don't overdress—and don't wear rubber suits to speed up weight loss! Wear as little as modesty and prudence dictate, but keep in mind that light-colored clothing reflects heat and that excessive tanning of the skin triggers the release of chemicals into the bloodstream that cause fatigue. Wear a cap to keep your head cooler. The cheapest headgear is a bandanna tied at each of the four corners and dipped in water. The weight of the knots keeps it snugly in place. Just as effective is dousing your head in water. City runners can splash themselves at hydrants or with hoses at friendly gas stations. Country runners can stick to shady roads. Try to run early or late and keep the runs short if need be. Drink as much as you can before, during, and after a run without, of course, making yourself sick. There is a danger during hot spells of incurring chronic dehydration since perceived thirst is not always an accurate indicator of the body's need for fluids. Not getting enough to drink is a quick way to wear yourself down. If you race even short distances in the heat—especially marathons—be realistic. A hot day is the worst time to try to run your fastest—just run to finish. No race is worth risking your health, ever.

The other major environmental consideration is air pollution, a serious, depressing, and unavoidable problem. It simply can't help our lungs to breathe in the wide spectrum of pollutants present in the air. There are only partial solutions to this problem. Try to run as far off to the side of busy streets or highways as possible. Avoid running through rush-hour congestion or heavily traveled streets. Run early or late. The most serious pollutant is carbon monoxide, which is colorless and odorless. It reduces the ability of the red blood cells to transport oxygen. Furthermore, it takes twelve to eighteen hours to be expelled from the system, and it has been shown to affect eye-hand coordination.

Good nutrition is as important a part of training and racing as any other factor. Miracle-mongering by devotees of different eating theories should be viewed with caution. If you don't know the fundamentals of good nutrition, learn them and incorporate whatever else you learn as it seems to make sense. There are a few general ideas to remember. Eating a wide variety of foods helps ensure proper intake of vitamins and minerals. Sugar and its cousins—honey, jam, dextrose, molasses, etc.—should be cut out or kept to a minimum. Alcohol should be avoided when you're in a state of deep fatigue immediately following a long run. Avoid oversalting food. The less processed your foods are and the less they need to be cooked, the less you need to eat and the easier it is for your body to extract needed nutrients. Minimum daily protein requirements are considerably lower than most people realize: about 70 to 100 grams (2½ to 3 ounces) a day. Protein consumed in excess of that level is broken down into urea and leaves the body in the urine, which is an expensive way to dispose of prime steak. A diet geared more toward vegetarianism with correspondingly less emphasis on meat and fat consumption seems to be the healthiest. The primary source of energy for muscles used in running is derived from glycogen, the end product of what we eat as carbohydrates (potatoes, pasta, fruits, vegetables, etc.). The last few days before a marathon should include ample amounts of carbohydrates in your diet.

Some runners use the carbohydrate loading diet. It is a difficult diet to get through, and there is some question as to its safety. For a first effort at a marathon, it doesn't seem necessary. If you do decide to try it, read up carefully on what is involved.

The last week before the marathon your running program should taper down to half of your average weekly mileage. During the last few days run just enough to stay limber. Get to the race in plenty of time and stop worrying about the extra miles you might have run. It's better to concentrate now on doing the best you can. Applying vaseline to areas of potential chafing—crotch, nipples, the outside of shoulder blades where the skin creases, and toes—

decreases the possibility of later incurring painful friction burns. Make sure your socks are wrinkle-free to avoid blisters. Never run in new shoes. Double-tie your laces. Drink a little fluid, stretch, and breathe deeply.

After the gun fires, let the mad ones dash off. Three hours is plenty of time for the tortoises to catch the hares—if they can. Even the veterans of many marathons get overexcited and go out faster than they should. That's no reason for you to follow their poor example. Run well at a comfortable pace for at least the first half of the race. You will constantly be wanting to go faster but don't. Even when 15 miles are done, 11 are left, which is a long way. If you have extra gas to burn in the latter stages of the race, you won't miss your chance. Don't listen to well-meaning spectators who tell you how far to the finish. They're never right. Take advantage of the water stations and stop to drink if you have to. A few seconds' loss will be more than regained. One thoroughly seasoned marathoner and ultramarathoner said that once in every race comes a point when you want to stop and wonder why you're out there. If you can just tough it through that bad patch, he said, it gets better, or the difficulty of it gets to feel normal.

Minimizing or exaggerating the struggle of a marathon doesn't make sense. The race you run will be your own. The satisfaction of running a marathon, the camaraderie you feel with others you run with on that day, and the satisfaction of finishing, no matter what place you take, is a very special feeling. It is worth working for. Good luck!

One of the unheralded many gets private congratulations.

Selected Readings

Anderson, Bob, and Henderson, Joe, eds. *Guide to Distance Running*. Mountain View, Calif.: World Publications, 1971.

Åstrand, Per-Olof, and Rodahl, Kaare. *Textbook of Work Physiology*. New York: McGraw-Hill, 1977.

Bowerman, William J., and Harris, W. E. *Jogging*. New York: Grosset & Dunlap, 1967.

Cooper, Kenneth H. *The New Aerobics*. New York: Bantam Books, 1970.

Glover, Bob, and Shepherd, Jack. *The Runner's Handbook*. New York: Penguin, 1978.

Henderson, Joe. *The Complete Marathoner*. Mountain View, Calif.: World Publications, 1978.

———. *Jog, Run, Race*. Mountain View, Calif.: World Publications, 1977.

————. *The Long Run Solution.* Mountain View, Calif.: World Publications, 1976.

————. *Run Gently, Run Long.* Mountain View, Calif.: World Publications, 1974.

Higdon, Hal. *Fitness After Forty.* Mountain View, Calif.: World Publications, 1977.

Hlavac, Harry F. *The Foot Book.* Mountain View, Calif.: World Publications, 1977.

Jackson, Ian. *Yoga and the Athlete.* Mountain View, Calif.: World Publications, 1975.

Lance, Kathryn. *Running for Health and Beauty: A Complete Guide for Women.* New York: Bobbs-Merrill, 1977.

Milvy, Paul, ed. *The Marathon: Physiological, Medical, Epidemiological and Psychological Studies.* New York: New York Academy of Sciences, 1977.

Sheehan, George A. *Dr. Sheehan on Running.* Mountain View, Calif.: World Publications, 1975.

————. *Running and Being.* New York: Simon & Schuster, 1978.

Ullyot, Joan. *Women's Running.* Mountain View, Calif.: World Publications, 1976.

van Aaken, Ernst. *The Van Aaken Method.* Mountain View, Calif.: World Publications, 1976.

Index

177